CW00661574

MY ANCESTOR WAS A RAILWAY WORKER

by Frank Hardy FSG

SOCIETY OF GENEALOGISTS ENTERPRISES LTD

Published by
Society of Genealogists Enterprises Limited
14 Charterhouse Buildings, Goswell Road, London EC1M 7BA
© The Society of Genealogists Enterprises and the author 2009.

ISBN: 978-1-907199-02-8

British Library Cataloguing in Publication Data
A CIP Catalogue record for this book is available from the British Library.

The Society of Genealogists Enterprises Limited is a wholly owned
subsidiary of the Society of Genealogists, a registered charity, no 233701.

About the Author

Frank Hardy was a professional railway civil engineer from 1959 to 2009. Having started his family history in 1977, he joined the Society of Genealogists in 1981. Since 1985, he has been helping regularly in the Library of the Society giving advice to users. He has also assisted with running the Family History Fairs at Westminster, Birmingham and latterly at Olympia. For the last five years he has assisted on the SoG stand at the Fairs at York and Gateshead, where he combines bookselling with giving genealogical advice.

Frank has been a member of the Computer, General Purposes and Library Committees as well as spending 15 years on the Executive Committee and Board of Trustees. He is a Fellow of the Society and is a Friend of the Society. As part of his work for the Society, since 2000 he has been project managing the indexing of the Shareholders' lists of the Great Western Railway, and expects that the finished work will be available for consultation during 2010.

Cover Image - © National Railway Museum/Science and Society Picture Library.

Graphic design and layout by Graham Collett.

CONTENTS

CONTENTS

ACKNOWLEDGMENTS

My thanks to all my colleagues during my railway career for their assistance in educating me about their work. I also thank Else Churchill for reminding me that one of the earliest railways was the often overlooked line between Canterbury and Whitstable.

CHAPTER ONE
Introduction

What are my qualifications to write a book like this? Well, I have been interested in railway operations and engineering work for as long as I can remember, and for the best part of 60 years have been interested in the history of the railways and their evolution. I have been a professional railwayman since 1959, predominantly as a bridge engineering manager, but with forays at the end of my career into safety and standards work and incident analysis in the bridge engineering field directed towards minimising train delays. My career has been one of hands-on management working as an engineer alongside bridge maintenance and construction gangs as well as managing a small drawing office and acting as a resident engineer responsible for every aspect of bridge reconstruction. This included the planning of train movements to get the new materials to site and to take away the old. As an extra, I have also been involved with directing track gangs and been in the small boy's dream situation of riding with train drivers and in some cases actually directing their movements during engineering works.

The sources used have been most of the books included in the Bibliography, combined with my own experience and reading.

All of this has given me a wide knowledge of who does what on the railway. Things did not change dramatically from the start of railways until the adoption of mechanisation on the track maintenance side in the 1970s and the availability of bigger and stronger lifting equipment of all kinds. I have witnessed the change from labour intensive work to machine intensive.

I started doing my family history back in 1977. Among the pieces of research I have done for the extended family was for the wife of a cousin. Her grandfather had been a signalman in Staffordshire, and had emigrated to New Zealand. The family had his New Zealand history, but Helen wanted to know more about his English railway career. This took me to The National Archives at Kew to search the North Staffordshire Railway staff records. After a bit of non-railway research, the railway track led me to Hereford. The results are shown in section 14 'Case Studies of a Railway Family', and will give some indication of what can be found for an ordinary railway employee in Victorian and Edwardian times.

The original title suggested for this book was 'My Ancestor was a Railwayman', but, during my research, I found that the first woman was employed on the railways around 1840. I also have been aware throughout my career that there are many people, both men and women, who were not employed by a railway company itself, but who spent major parts of their working lives on the railway working for a contractor.

A feature of railway history that comes through in books and records again and again is the dedication to duty of the ordinary lowly graded staff and, in the records of staff, one sees example after example of the enforcement of strict discipline. All this was based on simple principles, which still exist today, namely that the trains must run through safely and on time, but everyone had the safety rules drummed into them again and again at a yearly reading of rules by local supervisors, who in turn had the rules read to them by their managers.

The number of staff employed at any one time at its peak, between 1880 and 1910, was around 650,000. In the Victorian era, a job on the railway was seen as being for life, and the railway staff magazines are peppered with cases of staff receiving their long service awards of a watch or clock after 40 or 50 years service. Promotion was never easy and the only way of moving up through the ranks was often to move within the company to another location or to join a company which wanted experienced staff, perhaps to staff a new line. Railway employees were unusually mobile in the 19th and early 20th centuries compared to the general run of occupations in Britain.

What this book will tell you

The period covered by this book is primarily from the start of railways until 1948. The post 1948 era is lacking in archival material at the time of writing, but what applies before 1948 will still be generally correct as and when (or if) more recent records become available. Incidentally, as an aside, when looking at Victorian railway staff records, there is a similarity of terms used by the clerks of that era to those used by their successors in the 1970s and 80s. For example, you may find the phrase 'Advised for his future actions' appearing in disciplinary reports which is one step below a formal reprimand.

Throughout the book, '**CAUTIONARY NOTE**'s have been inserted, where advice is needed to highlight potential pitfalls when looking at the records.

My aim is to give a broad picture of the railway industry handling passengers and freight in Britain and to show what work the various people undertook. I will point you towards finding the solution to the problem that your ancestor was described on a Census return as a 'Fireman' and indicate where his records might be found.

Now the questions that spring to mind immediately on seeing that term in the Occupation column of a Census Return are:

◆ Was he a fireman riding on a shiny red fire engine rushing through the streets to put out a fire? This book probably will not help you unless he worked for a railway company in a big workshop complex, such as the works at Swindon.

◆ Was he a firemen stoking a stationary steam boiler in a factory? Again, this book probably will not help you unless he was in a railway works.

◆ Was he a fireman (stoker) on a ship? Sorry, this book will not help you, except if he served on a railway owned ship.

◆ Was he a locomotive fireman working for a railway, or was he employed in some sort of factory working on a small locomotive to move wagons around the factory complex? This book will help you in the first case, but not in the second case.

Similarly the terms 'Porter', 'Inspector', 'Boilersmith', 'Driver', 'Painter', 'Blacksmith', 'Cleaner', 'Guard', 'Fitter', 'Rivetter', 'Carter' can be ambiguous. These trades were used in other industries, and the researcher must not assume that there is a railway connection unless there is firm evidence pointing to the individual being a railway employee.

There are some trades which are only found on the railway and one or two other employers. What about a Signalman? Was he employed by a railway or by the Royal Navy or in the Army?

Apart from the Armed Forces and farming, there are very few occupations which cannot be found working on the railways. The only one that immediately comes to mind is undertaking; even so there are many railway staff who, through the years, have had to collect the remains of bodies involved in incidents on the railway.

I will also try to direct you towards items which can help you in your search and steer you away from items which do not include personal details. For example, the Census returns may supply addresses and when you look at a street map of the area, even if it is a few years before or after the date of the Census, a railway facility nearby may become obvious. You can then see if the staff records for that railway survive.

This book is intended to help you to understand the railway records that you may encounter in the search for your ancestor. Lists of staff records have been omitted as a complete listing is included in 'Was Your Grandfather a Railwayman?'.

I have included in the Bibliography a number of railway map books, as these are of great assistance to find which railway company could have employed your ancestor. Of the queries on railway ancestry that have been put to me over the last twenty years, the principal problem has been identification of the employing railway company.

The term 'main-line railways' is used to mean those railways which merged into the Big Four groups in 1923. Generally, they used the Stephenson or Standard Gauge of 4ft 8½ins.

Of course, there are many smaller companies which perhaps served a very limited area, or only lasted a few years before being absorbed into another company or even been driven out of business by competition. Some of these small companies such as the Talyllyn and Ffestiniog Railways in North Wales whilst today being regarded as 'Heritage Railways', have a long history starting from their foundation in the early to middle 19th century through to the 21st century.

Whilst this book is focussed towards records of the Main Line railways for England, Scotland and Wales, much of the information will be helpful when dealing with any railway staff records elsewhere, as many of the record types and terms used will be similar. The intention is to provide you with ideas for finding the individual in the railway records and to direct you to those sources which will add flesh to the bones.

This book may also help you in the circumstances where an ancestor, possibly not a railway employee, lived in a property which was affected by the construction of a railway. (See Deposited Plans in Section 13).

CAUTIONARY NOTE: It is rarely worth carrying out a speculative search without having the name and age of the individual. Some time spent carrying out research into the local railway history of the period will help establish where they might have been employed and by which company.

A potted history of the railway in Britain

The first public railway for coal traffic was opened in 1825 between Stockton on Tees and Darlington in County Durham. Previously there had been local plateways mainly serving mines, taking coal to the sea for loading onto ships to transport it to London. Most of these plateways were in the North-East of England. There was a notable exception in the Surrey Iron Railway, which ran from Wandsworth down the valley of the River Wandle to Croydon then into the North Downs near Redhill.

The first passenger and goods railways were the Canterbury & Whitstable and the Liverpool & Manchester Railway opened in 1830. The latter, on its opening day, achieved dubious fame by having the first case of a person being struck by a train and killed. I don't know what William Huskisson was like as an MP, but he has his place in history!

Gradually, a network of railways extended over the length and breadth of Britain from Penzance to Thurso and Great Yarmouth to Holyhead, operated by hundreds of companies great and small, famous and virtually unknown. Many mergers and creations of joint committees took place between 1840 and 1910, mainly for economic reasons to reduce wasted train mileage or to save station staff at junction stations. By having a Joint Committee to employ station staff, replication by two or more companies was avoided. The most famous case of a Joint Committee was that working Carlisle Citadel station, where 7 railway companies had a single station and staff to handle the trains passing through.

As a result railway history has effectively got a giant family tree showing all the relationships. As if the mergers were not enough, there were numerous working arrangements or 'running powers' where company A would say to company B 'If you let us run trains over your tracks from X to Y, we will let you run trains over our tracks from L to M'. This means that you may well find a company serving stations and having depots outside their normal operating area.

The North Eastern Railway ran from Berwick on Tweed to Edinburgh over the lines of the North British Railway, and the North British Railway worked south into Newcastle over the North Eastern Railway. In South London, the Great Western Railway had a large goods depot at South Lambeth in Battersea, and the London & North Western, Midland and Great Northern Railways had coal depots across from Battersea to Peckham and Dulwich, which were accessed by using running powers over the railways south of the River Thames.

> **CAUTIONARY NOTE:** When looking for an individual, make sure you are clear about the date range that you are searching and what the name of the railway company was at the relevant time. Here are a couple of examples:

- In 1846 the Leeds and Bradford Railway was opened; in 1852 it joined the Midland Railway; in 1923 it became part of the London Midland & Scottish Railway.

- In 1840 the Preston and Longridge Railway was opened; in 1852 it became part of the Fleetwood, Preston & West Riding Junction Railway; in 1860 it became part of the Lancashire & Yorkshire and London & North Western Joint Committee; in 1923 it became part of the London Midland & Scottish Railway.

A good railway history together with an Atlas like that produced by Col. Cobb is invaluable in sorting out these renamings and mergers.

In many railway books, initials are used to identify the railway rather that the full names. It is a lot simpler to write SE&CR, than South Eastern & London Chatham & Dover Joint Managing Committee. Even GWR instead of Great Western Railway is easier if you are in the know!

In the First World War, government intervention saw forced working arrangements in the national interest. The most famous arrangement was the running of the naval special trains from Euston and the coal fields to Invergordon and Thurso over the London & North Western, Caledonian, and Highland Railways to get crews and coal to the Home Fleet stationed at Invergordon and Scapa Flow. With many men conscripted the railway companies were extremely short of labour, and resorted to the previously unheard use of women for lighter duties. Inevitably, maintenance suffered, and major repairs were needed to trains and infrastructure. The costs would have bankrupted the railway industry and so the Railways Act of 1921 created four major companies, whose names were decided as:

- Great Western Railway

- London Midland & Scottish Railway

- London & North Eastern Railway

- Southern Railway

Almost every railway of the standard gauge of 4ft 8½ins was allocated by the Act to one of the 'Big Four', and the whole scheme came into effect on 1 January 1923 and is generally referred to in railway histories as the Grouping. Of the Big Four, only one retained an original name: this was the Great Western Railway which started its existence back in 1835 when it was formed to construct and operate a railway between London and Bristol, and gradually extended its sphere of operation to the area bounded by London, Penzance, Fishguard, Pwllheli, Chester and Birmingham. As a result the Great Western absorbed the smaller independent railways (mostly in the Welsh valleys) in its area rather than being an amalgamation of several large companies and a greater number of smaller companies.

Gradually the Big Four built bigger, faster and more luxurious trains and improved stations, until the advent of the Second World War, when for the second time in a century, the government took control of the railways for the benefit of the nation. Over the six years of the war, the whole system became run down and dilapidated, and effectively the Big Four companies were bankrupt. Again Parliament passed an Act (this time the Transport Act 1947), which nationalised the railways (along with canals and road transport, incidentally) on 1 January 1948. Almost the whole land transport industry – canals, buses, trains and road freight – came under the auspices of the British Transport Commission, of which the Railway Executive was part.

A few minor railways did not become included in the Grouping and Nationalisation that affected the main line railways in 1923 and 1948. The railways that were excluded, were (among others):

- Ffestiniog Railway

- Talyllyn Railway

- Post Office Railway (under Central London), which only carried mailbags and the staff were postmen.

- Ravenglass & Eskdale Railway

- Glasgow Subway (operated by Glasgow Corporation)

- Southwold Railway

- Hundred of Manhood & Selsey Tramway

- Romney Hythe & Dymchurch Railway

- Shropshire & Montgomeryshire Railway

Other minor railways such as the Ashover Railway, Lynton & Barnstaple Railway, Vale of Rheidol Railway and the Leek & Manifold Light Railway were absorbed into one or other of the Big Four railways in 1923 or shortly afterwards. The Kent & East Sussex Railway, and the East Kent Railway were nationalised in 1948.

CAUTIONARY NOTE: The name of a railway company does not always relate to the places actually served. The Manchester & Milford Railway served neither Manchester nor Milford Haven, and merely ran for a few miles in Central Wales.

Since 1948, the railway industry has survived despite various degrees of government interference (by people who have no practical experience), not to mention reorganisation after reorganisation, privatisation and refranchising of the operating companies. To quote Gerard Fiennes, a railway General Manager in the 1960s, 'When you reorganise, you bleed'. The various reorganisations over the period from 1970 to 2008 have effectively ensured that it will be difficult to trace the career history of a modern-day railway person. As far as those people employed by railway contractors are concerned, I suspect that it will be impossible to trace them in 50 years time, especially when they were employed by a small company.

CAUTIONARY NOTE: If you are trying to trace the railway career of anyone since the Second World War, there are no records available as they remain within the railway industry both for pension purposes and for handling claims for injuries and diseases resulting from railway employment.

In my career, which spanned a few months short of 50 years, I was employed by the British Transport Commission, British Railways Board, Railtrack, two commercial recruitment agencies and, finally, Network Rail and yet I have always worked within railway offices. Even now, I am still effectively on the railway 'strength' as I receive my railway pension. I know that you will not be able to trace my staff history, as it was found to have been destroyed when I took early retirement in 1995; all that survived was the last four years or so on a computer print out, and this was the case in general at the end of the 20th century as managers found when seeking staff details for people coming up for promotional interviews. I do not envy the genealogist of the future when they are trying to find railway staff records, because there will be nothing accessible from the employers.

How many railway people?

This is a difficult question to answer. It is suggested by Christian Wolmar in his book 'Fire and Steam' that in 1901 there were 650,000 people employed by the railway companies. I think this must have been somewhere near the maximum number employed at any one time. My reasoning is that between 1830 and 1900 the number of lines was growing and services were expanding, particularly becoming more frequent.

The introduction of shorter working weeks down to an 8 hours day did slow down the drop in numbers. In the second half of the 20th century there was a gradual decline, because electrification eliminated the need for locomotive firemen, and faster trains meant that an individual member of train crew could do more work within their turn of duty.

One also has to take into account that many employees worked within the industry for 30, 40 or even 50 years, when making an assessment of the total number of individuals who were employed between 1830 and 1948. On this basis, I estimate that there must be at least 2 million individuals, and possibly as many as 3 million people, who were employed at one time or another from 1830 up to 1948.

What records can be found?

Most of the surviving staff records are to be found at The National Archives (TNA) at Kew or, for Scottish companies, at the Scottish Archives at Edinburgh. Regrettably, when one looks at the lists of holdings for the TNA, only a small proportion of railway companies staff records have survived. Staff records for just over 100 companies out of over 900 individual railways exist according to the TNA lists.

Of these 100 companies, you may find that the particular departmental records have not survived, or that the volumes available are too early or too late to show your ancestor.

All is not lost, however. For the vast majority of companies, there are some records which may show individuals, and I have tried to show some of these in the rest of this section.

Staff records

Staff and salary registers. These will generally relate to a particular department or depot. Some are indexed or have a name index in a separate volume. If there is no index, the entries were probably made in order of the date of appointment.

Whilst most staff records are at TNA, some county record offices hold some registers (e.g Cheshire Record Office has 17 registers relating to staff of railways within Cheshire). TNA advise searching the internet using the A2A (Access to Archives) website.

Where companies amalgamated or were taken over, it will be necessary to seek records for both the original company, and the new company. In many cases, the old company staff registers continued in use for several years until the book was full.

Personnel files. It might be worth searching the files held at TNA to see if any general files have been retained with details of staff postings, accidents, commendations and disciplinary actions taken. These files may be arranged by depot or by department. Lists of joiners, leavers and those granted pensions may exist for a particular company. These would be located within the RAIL class for the particular company.

CAUTIONARY NOTE: The dates quoted on files and registers can be misleading. The dates given may be for the date of birth of the first person listed or his date of entering railway service, and the last date could be the date when the last person died. A register purporting to be from, say, 1840 to 1900, may not contain every member of staff employed between those dates. Sometimes two or more registers cover a particular year and all relevant registers need to be searched. Alphabetical sequence is often lacking as entries were made as staff arrived.

Contained within the surviving documents at TNA are a few apprenticeship indentures, photographs and testimonials. As well as the staff records listed by Tom Richards, there are other items which mention individuals and these are listed below.

The only staff records held by the Society of Genealogists are a set of record cards for some staff at York Locomotive depot. There are about 2400 cards for drivers, firemen and maintenance staff. It appears that the cards were compiled by the London and North Eastern Railway in the period 1920-1948. They include staff taken on by the North Eastern Railway in the 1880s, and some of the information appears to have been copied from a previous set of records.

Figure 1

on page 12 shows the front of the card for James Acomb, who was born in 1862 and started work at Tyne Dock shed in 1887 as a fireman. It then records his pay increases and promotions until his retirement in 1930 aged 68. The lower part shows the result of eye tests, some of which were conducted at Pilmoor, where a signal gantry had been erected beside the line specifically for carrying out eye testing. The pay details are not recorded on this card after 1919, and I assume that he was paid at a standard rate for his grade and seniority.

Figure 2

on page 13 is the reverse of the card for James Acomb, and details his disciplinary record. There is a commendation for working during a partial strike in December 1912. Again there are no details after 1917, so either he became a reformed character or there was a separate series of cards for the later period.

Figure 3

on page 14 show the front of the card for Ernest James Allison who was a boilersmith. He was born in 1884, and first employed in 1911 at York. Interestingly, the pay rates for the period of World War 2 shows a basic rate and a bonus rate. This bonus rate was, I believe, a rise granted to allow for the extra cost of living without the need to negotiate basic rates with the unions. There is a badge number shown, and this relates, almost certainly, to a wartime badge issued to those people who were in reserved occupations. A railway boilersmith would fall into this category being involved with essential work for the war effort although not conscripted.

Figure 4

on page 14 show the reverse of the card for Ernest James Allison, and details various disciplinary actions taken against him.

The cards are available on request to the Library staff in the Lower Library at the Society, giving the surname of interest. However, please be sure that the person worked for the Mechanical Engineers at the Locomotive Depot at York as a driver, fireman or repair staff.

London & North Eastern Railway.—Loco.' Running Department. | LR 7690

FOOTPLATE STAFF *Certificate* Staff No. 206

Name *Acomb James* Date of Birth *14.7.62.* Seniority Date *29-11-81.*

Entered Service: Date *29-11-81.* Grade *Fireman*

Height (Stockinged Feet) ___ ft. ___ ins. Date examined _____ Date of exception from Unemployment Insurance. *8/1/30*

___ ft. ___ ins. Date examined _____

Passed as Fireman _____ Passed as Driver _____

STAFF RECORD.

Date.	Grade.	Depot.	Rates of Pay.				Date.	Grade.	Depot.	Rates of Pay.			
			Cleaner.	Fireman.	Driver. Shunting, etc.	Main Line.				Cleaner.	Fireman.	Driver. Shunting, etc.	Main Line.
29 11 81	Fireman	Tyne Dock		3/4			41030	Retired (Age Limit)					
24 7 82	"	"		3/6				68					
24 11 82	"	"		3/10									
22 8 84	"	York		3/10									
11 12 84	"	"		4/-									
31 12 85	"	"		4/6									
29 11 89	"	"		4/9									
9 6 93	Driver	"			6/6								
14 12 93	"	"			6/-								
27 10 97	"	"			6/6								
22 10 98	"	"			7/-								
9 6 00	"	"			7/6								
18 8 19	"	"			15/-								

EYESIGHT AND MEDICAL EXAMINATIONS.

Date.	Reason for Examination.	Result.			Colour Vision.	Physical Fitness Remarks.	Date.	Reason for Examination.	Result.			Colour Vision.	Physical Fitness Remarks.
		R.E.	L.E.	Both.					R.E.	L.E.	Both.		
5 6 93		6/6	6/6		Good		25 7 25		6/24	6/36	6/24	N	
19 6 03		6/6	6/6	6/6			28 8 25	Eyesight	Passed Train Test				
28 9 10		6/12	6/9	6/9	N.		8 7 27		6/24	6/36	6/24	N	
27 5 13		6/12	6/12	6/12			14 10 27	Eyesight	Passed Train Test				
6 5 15		6/12	6/12	6/12			23 8 29		6/60	6/36	6/36.	N	
31 5 17		6/18	6/18	6/12			27 9 29	Eyesight	Passed Train Test				
15 6 23		6/24	6/24	6/24									
17 23	Eyesight	Passed Train Work											

Special Remarks: (Including references to Injuries)

Figure 1

Date of Occurrence.	Punishment or Gratuity.	PARTICULARS.	Reference to Papers.
19·11·87	Fine 1/-	Not seeing the face nuts were secure on Eg 1463. pusher fell off into Main Station at Durham	
22·5·88	Caution	Late	
7·10·90	Fine 1/-	Having Eg 239 off rails in York Yard thro inattention to points	
22·5·99	Caution	Late	
3·1·06	Susp 4 Days	Passing signal at danger at Selby when in charge of L.E. 2009.	
6·9·07	Fine 3/6.	Not keeping a good look out when in charge of Eg 1810 resulting in its colliding with Eg 570 at Ferryhill	
31·7·08	Caution	Omitting to stop at Thirsk with 10.33a Hull-Dover Eg 703	
11·8·08	Susp 3 Days	Mistaking signal at Leeds Cabin York causing Eg 134 to be derailed	
20·7·14	Susp 1 Day	Overrunning Inner Home Signal at danger at Darlington South Cabin whilst working 9.40a E.R. Leeds-Hull	
25·3·15	St. Paul	Failing to bring 4.50p E.P. car hall Eg 364 to rest in time to avoid colliding with rear portion of 6.34p E.P. York & Dover on No 74 Platform York Stn	
24·3·17	St. Paul	Allowing Eg 2164 working 5.30p E.P. car York to come into slight collision with a standing pass train on Down Station causing damage to rear van	
	Bonus £ 1-11-0	For working engine into the affected area during hail storm Dec/12.	

LNER 3060/3.27 5,000.   London & North Eastern Railway. - Loco.' Running Department.

LR 7691A

SHED (WORKSHOP) STAFF. 307   Staff No. 80

Name _Allison_   Date of Birth _14·8·84._   BC 9/5/29

BA896 84354 Ernest James   STAFF RECORD.

Date.	Grade.	Depot.	Rate. Base.	Rate. Bonus.	Date.	Grade.	Depot.	Rate. Base.	Rate. Bonus.
Apl 7/11	Boilerman and Crossland	YORK							
Nov 1/1912	Boilersmith	YORK /10	51/-	16/6					
9, 3 42	"	"	51/-	32/6					
1 2 48	"	"	84/6	31/6					
14 8 49	Retired								

Special Remarks (Including references to Injuries : —

Figure 3

PARTICULARS OF PUNISHMENTS, &c. (Black), REWARDS AND COMMENDATIONS (Red).

Date of Occurrence.	Punishment or Gratuity.	PARTICULARS.	Reference to Papers.
22 10 33	Personal Reprimand	Not screwing the lead plug properly into the plate of Eng. 2346	G 7624
24 3 34	Caution	Not reporting sediments in boiler of Eng. 926 when cleaning the same	B.E.
15 11 35	Caution	Unsatisfactory workmanship in connection with mud hole door of Eng. 2482	G 7376
15 11 47	Caution	Abs.	G 15-11-47
1 1 49	"		G 1.1.49
28 12 48	1/2 Late	at Dentist	
20 10 47	1/2 Late	no reply	

MEDICAL EXAMINATIONS.

Date.	Reason for Examination.	Physical Fitness. Remarks.		Date.	Reason for Examination.	Physical Fitness. Remarks.
14 11 4?	Not prev. exd.	<6/60 <6/60 <6/60 with glasses 6/9 6/9 6/9 fit				

Figure 4

14

Accident Reports by the Board of Trade and Ministry of Transport and Civil Aviation made by His/Her Majestys' Railway Inspectorate. A set of reports is found at TNA. These cover the major incidents involving passenger fatalities and a small number of other significant incidents. If your ancestor was a train driver involved in a major train collision such as the one at Harrow in 1952, the name will be mentioned with some detail of what actions they took at the time. Anyone who gave evidence at the public inquiry will be mentioned together with a summary of their evidence. The reports do not cover staff injuries and fatalities such as falling off a ladder or being hit by a train unless a passenger was also killed. If, however, you have definite proof that someone was involved, although otherwise unhurt, these reports and the Annual Report can give useful background about an event.

CAUTIONARY NOTE: The Annual Reports of the Railway Inspectorate do not mention any names and are primarily concerned with statistics. They will tell you how many people fell off ladders for the year under review, but not who fell.

Directors' Meetings and Minute Books (English companies at TNA, Scottish companies at Scottish Archives). Numerous committees existed for each company, and these can give a good picture of the company's activities at a particular time. Books from the early days of the company may be informative regarding the names of contractors who carried out work. The earliest employees may be mentioned, with the date of starting work. Once the railway had started running trains, some minute books may mention meritorious service or refer to disciplinary actions taken regarding individual staff. In other cases there are references to individuals being appointed together with their pay rates. Long serving members of staff who retired were often granted a pension by their employer, and this may be recorded in a minute in the days before pension funds being formed.

CAUTIONARY NOTE: Once a company employed more than a couple of hundred people, the Directors would delegate the responsibility of hiring and firing staff down the management chain, so that a Station Master, even of a small station, would have an establishment set for his station and could hire and fire staff within that establishment without referring appointments back to the Board of Directors for approval. Therefore you are unlikely to find low graded staff in the minutes of (say) the Great Western Railway after its early years.

Local newspapers (found at the British Library or in local archives and libraries). If the date of an event such as an accident, death or retirement affecting the railway or its servants, the local newspaper may have reported details. If there was a fatality (of staff or a member of the public), there will have been a Coroner's Inquest and this will almost certainly have been reported locally (This may lead you to the Inquest Report in a local Record Office). There will also be newspaper reports of floods and earth slips or landslides affecting transport, where perhaps an individual made strenuous efforts to stop trains running into an obstruction.

Railway enthusiast magazines (full runs are held at the British Library): particularly the *Railway Magazine* which has been published since 1897 and contains numerous historical articles about specific sections of railways lines. These articles will often detail the opening and closing dates for lines and stations. The *Railway Magazine* also carried potted biographies of managers (generally Station Masters or above) who retired or were being promoted; a very few Top Link drivers were also featured in the 1940s. Started more recently are *Backtrack* and *British Railways Illustrated* which frequently have good quality historical articles and, less frequently, a few biographical articles. *Steam World* generally contains one article each month recounting the experiences of an individual, frequently drivers and firemen, Some of the monthly periodicals seen on bookshop shelves frankly are not worth buying unless you want to know details of the history of locomotive no 1234, or whether there were 20 or 21 rivets in a part of its anatomy!

Railway enthusiast books (some held at National Railway Museum). If you are lucky enough to have a photograph of your ancestor who was a driver or fireman that shows a locomotive, it should be possible to find an illustration of the type of locomotive on which they worked. Published histories of locomotive classes would be worth consulting for illustrations.

Railway staff magazines (copies held at British Library (Newspaper Library), TNA or National Railway Museum). Started around 1900 and carry lists and details of staff retirements and some promotions, but generally staff are not indexed in any detail. The annual index will have an entry for retirements, with the relevant page number in each monthly issue. The *British Railways Magazine* was published from 1949 monthly in six regional editions, and gave details of many staff movements for the region covered by that edition. More recently, *Railnews* covers industry wide events, but no general listing of promotions and retirements have been published since the mid 1980s when the information was deemed to be commercially sensitive or confidential (I suspect the true reason was actually that there was little interest as the average length of service for individuals was rapidly shortening as people moved to and from companies on and off the railway).

Histories of particular railways. These will generally be found in reference libraries of the area, although some of the more prominent companies such as the Great Western Railway may be found more widely. (For a listing of material that has been published see Ottley: Bibliography - included in the Bibliography section at the end of this book.)

Year Books. There was a Railway Year Book published from about 1897. This is a useful publication if your ancestor was a Director or a Chief Officer of a Railway Company, and has about 250-300 potted biographies of these people. In addition it can give you a general overview of the company concerned, but it will not enable you to trace your ancestor if he/she was an employee below managerial grade.

> **CAUTIONARY NOTE:** As far as I can tell from perusal of the 1922 edition, the only people listed are the departmental heads. There are no station masters, signalmen or drivers listed, and so for the average person it is of no use in tracing railway ancestors.

What records will not be found

Almost certainly you will not find any connection between records if an individual changed jobs and moved between companies or perhaps even between the districts of a single company. My experience (admittedly limited) suggests that home addresses were not generally recorded in staff registers. A staff register for the first employer will merely record that the individual left the service, and that for the new employer will just give a date of joining.

Staff records after 1923 are very thin on the ground: out of 40 pages of records listed by Tom Richards, about 4 pages refers to material from the 1923-1948 period and less than 1 page refers to post 1948 material.

What information do you need to start looking

To search the records successfully, one needs to know a name, a place and occupation and you will need to start your search outside the railway records. Unless you know a name, it is impossible to locate the record of an individual. Remember that the general rules of genealogical searching apply – names may be spelt in a different way (Smith and Smythe will be separated in any alphabetical listing) because a clerk misheard the name or misread a name on another document. The man you know of as Tony was actually, officially perhaps, Anthony (or vice versa). If at first you don't find the person you are seeking bear in mind the possible variations.

The starting point must be where the person was living, and this is almost the easiest part of the search. With the advent of the indexes to the Census Returns for 1911 and earlier, it is possible to search for a named individual, and with an uncommon name you will in a short time have the census entry on screen in front of you. With the Censuses from 1851 to 1911, the occupation will be given: perhaps it just says 'Fitter', or if you are in luck 'Railway Fitter', or the answer that you really want 'Railway Fitter (Great Western Railway). Always look at the occupations of the heads of household in the street and the general area. If there are a large proportion of railway people there, it is likely that the area is one where the railway has built the housing or that there is a substantial railway presence nearby. With the address, you can then look at local Ordnance Survey maps to see which railway company or companies served the area, and so narrow the number of possible sources for information about your individual.

Are there any family papers or artifacts which prove a railway connection? Has something like a gold watch or clock been presented for long service or as a retirement gift with a brass plaque affixed? Perhaps there is a certificate which commemorates especially good service lurking somewhere?

It is worth remembering that staff moved around on promotion, either within their own company or because they saw a job opportunity elsewhere. It is possible that you may find the same individual in the records of two or more companies. Perhaps a move was because a new railway line was starting up and recruiting staff.

The maps listed in the bibliography may help to pinpoint the company, as some areas were dominated by a single company; for example if someone was a railway man living in Newcastle upon Tyne or Gateshead, it is nearly a certainty that they were working for the North Eastern Railway. However if they were in Battersea, in South London it could be the London Chatham & Dover Railway, the London Brighton & South Coast Railway or the London & South Western Railway; there were also small groups of staff in the area employed by the Midland Railway and Great Western Railway. At Willesden in North West London, locomotive sheds of the Great Western Railway and London & North Western Railway were in close proximity, with the Cricklewood shed of the Midland Railway within walking distance. (See Section 15 for a listing of towns with the railways serving them.)

Remember that, before the Second World War, railway staff would generally live within walking distance of their place of work.

A useful resource for finding which railway company may have employed your ancestor is *Railway Ancestors* by David Hawkins. In one of the appendices, he has listed, by county, all railway companies running through a county. In another appendix, he has listed all the railway companies, and, most importantly which of them have railway staff records that survive.

One thing that needs to be borne in mind is that a very limited amount of new material comes to light from time to time. This material is a result of either recataloguing of collections, or of items held privately being deposited in archives. However it must be made clear that it is probably a matter of, at most, 50 or so items a year nationally.

Do you have an old photograph of your ancestor taken on the railway? If so the background may give a clue to the location and company who employed the person. A locomotive type or carriage would indicate the company, while a building can be a good clue to the company or even the place where the photograph was taken. It would be necessary to find someone with the necessary specialist railway historical knowledge to positively identify the detail, but some magazines in the railway enthusiast press do publish 'puzzle' pictures from time to time, and frequently an answer is forthcoming from a reader (I hasten to add that I am NOT one of the experts in that field).

CAUTIONARY NOTE: Beware of assuming that because a person lived in, say, Reading, they MUST have worked for the Great Western Railway. The South Eastern Railway (later the South Eastern & Chatham Joint Managing Committee) had a station and engine shed at Reading. An article in a family history magazine said that a signalman at Reading would have worked for the Great Western. I beg to differ, as there were at least 2 signal boxes at Reading worked by the South Eastern. There are numerous other locations where a similar situation arose (see Section 17 for a listing).

There is no general index for railway staff, so the records for each company need to be searched, and even then, there is not always an index to the material that is available. Sometimes, each volume has an index and in other cases, the index volumes cover two or three of the staff registers.

At the time of writing, this cannot be done on the Internet in the comfort of your own home; it is necessary to visit The National Archives at Kew or whichever other record office holds the material in which you might find the individual.

The National Archives have plans for digitising many of the records that they hold, but at the time of writing no date has been suggested for when the railway staff records will be appearing on line.

Women on the Railway

The earliest mention that I have seen to a woman working on a railway dates from around 1840, but I am not clear about who was her employer. It may have been a local initiative by the Station Master rather than the railway company itself. In any event, the first women employed were as attendants in ladies' waiting rooms at stations, probably initially in the First Class rooms. Their duties would have been to keep the rooms clean and to assist ladies.

Gradually women became accepted in places like refreshment rooms as waitresses where meals were served at table.

It was with the First World War that women became employed more widely but only in lighter duties – clerical posts particularly – to replace men who had gone to join the army and navy. In the later stages of the war, a few gangs were formed of women to clean locomotives, and a number were trained as guards, porters, ticket collectors and as signal*men*. In some cases, their grade was Woman Guard, etc.

The trade unions reluctantly accepted that women had to be employed, but it appears that the unions did their best to ignore the facts and pretend the women did not exist.

Come the Armistice in 1918, and the return of men from military service, almost all the women were, to put it bluntly, dismissed from the railway service, with minimal notice as they were seen as being temporary staff. A few women continued to be employed; frequently they were from railway families and probably, I suspect, were protected from harassment by their relatives. The jobs they undertook were mainly white-collar, but some wives married to crossing keepers acted as the crossing keeper for meal breaks and the like. In some cases this was officially recognised, but not always, with the woman frequently being unpaid.

Over the years between the two world wars, women came into the engineering drawing offices and also worked on the many telephone switchboards across the country. The female switchboard operators tended to do the day shifts with men doing the night shifts, but gradually the distinction was eroded.

With the Second World War, women were much more accepted, and as well as carrying out office duties, some were trained as guards, porters, ticket collectors and signalmen, along with medium sized gangs of locomotive cleaners and even track maintenance staff. Although, as after the First World War, many were dismissed in 1945/6 as men returned, a number stayed on in the offices. By the end of the 20th century there was no job on the railway which women did not do, and with the advent of equipment to do the heavy lifting, there are a substantial number of women employed at all levels throughout the industry.

There are two books which cover the subject in greater detail:

♦ *Railwaywomen: Exploitation, betrayal and triumph in the workplace* by Helena Wojtczak

♦ *The Fair Sex – Women and the Great Western Railway* by Rosa Matheson

Railways that never were

In the 1840s and 1850s there were many competing proposals for railway lines – there were at least three schemes proposed between London and Brighton for example. Later in the early part of the 20th century there were schemes promoted for light railways and all these schemes had to have the necessary Deposited Plans and Books of Reference prepared and submitted to Parliament, so if your ancestor lived on the route of one of these abortive schemes, it could be worth looking to see if any records survive. I have seen a copy of the Deposited Plans for a line from Lenham to Faversham in Mid Kent, which was found when we were moving offices many years ago.

The Plans and Books can be found in the Parliamentary Archives and Local Record Offices.

CHAPTER TWO
Construction of New Railways

Almost without exception the construction of new railways was not carried out by individuals directly employed by railway companies. Instead all work was contracted out to companies specialising in earth moving, tunnelling and bridge construction. Names that spring to mind for the early Victorian period are Firbank, Thomas Brassey and Samuel Peto. Thomas Brassey was said to be the most successful contractor of his generation and died in 1870, shortly after his company had completed the construction of the extension of the Midland Railway from Bedford to London (St Pancras). Even today, the major works are carried out by contractors. Over the years most of the large Civil Engineering Contractors have carried out contracts for the railway – the West Highland Extension line from Fort William to Mallaig was the first major use of concrete for construction of big bridges by 'Concrete Bob' MacAlpine.

In the 19th century, the work was carried out by huge gangs of navvies, aided by horses and carts, and the navvies would move along the route as sections were completed. They caused major upsets to rural communities, and would build shanty towns if no other living accommodation was available. The 'navigators' (or navvies) were originally the men who excavated the navigations (or canals) around the country, but as canal construction died out it was superseded by railway construction, and the men moved from one form of transport to another, taking their name with them.

Far from being a rabble, the navigators were a highly skilled, elite, force who did the hardest work such as tunnelling, and excavation, using gunpowder as necessary, and they did prodigious amounts of work. To match their work, they ate and drank heavily, and their strength was far superior to the ordinary labourer, who would work on a farm when needed, or move to other work when farming had no use for them. Particularly large contingents of navvies came from Scotland and Ireland, as well as from Lancashire and Yorkshire.

There are sketches of the excavation of Tring cutting in Hertfordshire showing barrow runs up the slopes of the cut, with a horse on the top level pulling a barrow, steered by a navvy, up the timber run. The navvys would excavate the ground, load the barrows and then take the excavated material to where it was wanted and then tip it to form an embankment. Imagine the human effort required to excavate a cutting 2 miles long, 40 feet deep and 30 feet wide at track level; there is no doubt that the navvies earned their rations. It has been calculated that the London & Birmingham Railway required 25,000 million cubic feet of earth and rock to be moved by 20,000 men in 5 years.

Of course there were also bridges to be constructed over and under the railway. To give some idea of the work involved, the viaduct that carries the Euston to Glasgow and Liverpool line across the Weaver River is 500 yards long, 65 feet above the river and consists of 20 sandstone arches. This took 2 years to build in the 1840s and is still in use today. It is claimed that the construction of this viaduct was achieved without any fatality, which suggests that it was unusual not to have killed someone. The material used for bridges have varied over the years and this means that different trades were employed according to the material in use.

In the earliest days, brick or stone masonry was the normal construction material and all bridges were of arch form and many survive today under much heavier loading. Where there is natural stone available, this would be quarried for use in bridge building. If no local stone was available, especially where clay was available nearby, bricks were used. Local brick kilns were set up, often using clay excavated from the cuttings.

Around 1850, cast iron became popular, but there were a number of spectacular failures (e.g. the Tay Bridge at Dundee) compounded by its brittle nature. Wrought iron took over as the material for girder bridges from around 1870, and this allowed the construction of longer bridge spans. The final developments occurred in the 20th century with the use of rolled steel and concrete.

At the peak of railway construction around 1850, it has been estimated that there were some 200,000 workers around the country. It was hard and dangerous work, and deaths were commonplace. Towards the end of the 19th century, steam driven diggers became available, along with temporary track, which eased the work of the navvies. The Newton Collection of photographs housed at Leicester Libraries shows the construction of the Great Central Railway from Sheffield to London (Marylebone) between 1895 and 1902.

An additional complication arises because, generally a main contractor would be appointed, and in turn they would contract some or all of the work to sub-contractors, would supply the actual workforce. In turn, sub contractors might employ smaller contractors. The main contractor was the only one with whom the railway had dealings, and would only have a relatively small management and supervisory team involved with the contract.

Where contractors were employed, tracing individuals employed is just about impossible, as the civil engineering industry has always been noted for employing casual labour; manpower is recruited as needed on a 'job and finish' basis and there is rarely any continuity of employment except for the supervisory staff, and even they move on as the jobs move. I have known men who have worked for a number of different contractors on works where I was the supervising engineer for British Railways, and from conversation with older men, it was apparent this mobility was considered to be the normal, not to say, traditional thing.

Tunnels

Tunnel construction was highly skilled and dangerous work carried out by teams of miners and bricklayers. The miners would start by excavating a short length of a few yards and the bricklayers would lay the arched brickwork on a timber formwork. After the brick mortar had set and the ground was supported, the whole process would start over for the next few feet right through the tunnel. Work would normally start from both ends and from shafts sunk at about 400 yard intervals along the line of the tunnel.

Where the tunnel passed through natural stone, it may well have been left unlined if the stone was stable, and there are tunnels in use today where this is the case.

Regrettably collapses of the unhardened brickwork or unsupported ground were fairly commonplace during construction. Conditions were very poor, and many tunnels were running with water percolating through the ground. I have found records of the tunnel construction in Directors' Committee minute books which helped to explain some of the modern day problems in tunnels in Southern England.

Stations

Basically a small or medium sized station would use all the normal trades that are to be found in house building. The very large stations like Paddington, King's Cross, Manchester, would have been constructed by civil engineering contractors. For example, the large iron arch ribs for the train shed at St Pancras in London were cast by the Butterley Company at Ripley in Derbyshire and brought down to London and erected in 1868 using timber scaffolding. As an aside, the same firm was responsible for fabricating and erecting many replacement bridges for the railway over the next 125 years, and as part of my duties in the 1970s and 1980s, I would have to go to the Butterley works to inspect the progress of work on the fabrication of steelwork for new bridge spans.

Signalling

New signalling installations could be carried out by either the railway's own staff from the Signal Engineering Department or by specialist contractors such as W. J. Sykes, Saxby & Farmer, Mackenzie & Holland or the Westinghouse Brake and Signal Company. Where the work was carried out by railway staff, the majority of the equipment was supplied by one of the contractors.

Signal boxes were manufactured both by railway companies and by contractors – in each case there were distinctive styles, and a photograph of a signalman standing outside 'his' box might enable a railway expert to identify the railway company who employed the man simply by looking at the architecture.

Two exceptions to the use of contractors were the Great Western Railway which had its own signal works at Reading (but brought in iron castings) and the London & North Western Railway which manufactured all the equipment needed by that company in their works at Crewe.

CHAPTER THREE
Building the Trains

In the early days of railways, the original trains themselves were built often by small firms who had developed from the engineering works that manufactured stationary engines for use at the start of the Industrial Revolution. There was a gradual changeover from the stationary engines to the manufacture of railway engines, carriages and wagons.

Until around 1930, except for the very big railway companies, many locomotives and about 50% of the carriages and wagons were manufactured off railway property. Since 1965, Britain's railways have reverted to acquiring rolling stock from manufacturers such as Brush at Loughborough and Siemens and Alstom in Europe and very recently Hitachi in Japan. There is one of the old railway workshop sites still constructing carriages at Derby. The most recent freight locomotives, now a class nearly 500 strong, are built by EMD in London – no, not England but in Ontario, Canada.

Workshop sites where major construction of trains by the railways themselves took place included:

Location	Locomotives	Carriages	Wagons
Swindon	Yes	Yes	Yes
Ashford (Kent)	Yes	Yes	Yes
Brighton	Yes	Yes	Yes
Lancing		Yes	Yes
Eastleigh (Hants)	Yes	Yes	Yes
Nine Elms (London)	Yes	Yes	Yes
Derby	Yes	Yes	Yes
Doncaster	Yes	Yes	Yes
Horwich (Lancs)	Yes	Yes	Yes
Darlington	Yes	Yes	Yes
Glasgow	Yes	Yes	Yes
York	Yes	Yes	Yes
Crewe	Yes	Yes	Yes
Shildon			Yes
Stratford (London)	Yes	Yes	Yes
Gorton	Yes	Yes	Yes
Wolverton		Yes	Yes

Private companies supplying trains to the railway included:

Company	Locomotives	Carriages	Wagons
Sharp Roberts of Manchester; became Sharp Stewart in 1852, moved to Glasgow in 1888	Yes		
North British, Glasgow. Formed from Neilson, Sharp Stewart and Dubs	Yes		
Birmingham Carriage & Wagon		Yes	Yes
Gloucester Carriage & Wagon		Yes	Yes
Cravens, Sheffield		Yes	Yes
Robert Stephenson, Newcastle, later Darlington	Yes		
Head Wrightson	Yes		
Avonside Engine Co, Bristol	Yes		
Vulcan Foundry, Newton le Willows	Yes		
Neilson, Glasgow	Yes		
Kitson, Leeds	Yes	Yes	Yes
Hunslet, Leeds	Yes		
Beyer Peacock, Manchester	Yes		
Dubs, Glasgow	Yes		
Hurst Nelson, Motherwell		Yes	Yes
Charles Roberts, Wakefield		Yes	Yes
Peckett, Bristol	Yes (small)		
Hudswell-Clarke, Leeds	Yes (small)		

CHAPTER FOUR
Maintaining the Infrastructure

The maintenance of the railway was the responsibility of the Engineer. Initially he was responsible for all the infrastructure, but gradually with increasing complexity, the Signalling and Telecommunications and the Electrical Engineers were appointed to look after their specialities.

Earthworks

With railways needing to maintain the flattest gradient possible, there are many miles of cuttings where the railway runs lower than the surrounding ground, or, conversely, embankments where the railway runs many feet above the natural ground level. In both situations the slopes are prone to slip downwards as a result of rainfall. This required the local track maintenance gangs to undertake ditching and draining to reduce the risk of earthslips. At some locations it became necessary to construct large retaining structures to maintain the railway formation.

Bridges

Every time the line of a railway came to a road, either a public highway or a farm track, it was necessary for a bridge to be constructed, unless the railway was running at the natural level of the ground. Bridges were and

are made from brick, stone, cast or wrought iron or steel. Brick and stone bridges are arched, whereas the metal bridges tend to be straight girders. Cast iron bridges are now extremely rare, due to the brittle nature of cast iron under cyclic loadings as are produced by trains passing over the bridge.

Gangs of bricklayers and masons were employed to repair the arch bridges and brick supports whilst ironworkers were employed to repair and renew the iron and steel bridges.

The generic description 'ironworkers' included the following trades:

- Platers – marked out and cut wrought iron and steel to the engineers' designs and then drilled the holes for the rivets and bolts.

- Rivetters – placed and drove the red-hot iron rivets to secure plates together, using hammers (originally by hand, but later hydraulic driven machines) to force the rivets into place to make a very secure fastening.

- Erectors – the men who manoeuvred the metal parts into position and bolted them together during the erection of a metal bridge on site.

Tunnels

Tunnel maintenance was carried out by teams of bricklayers repointing the mortar joints in the brickwork of the tunnel itself and in the ventilation shafts extending up though the ground to the surface. The pointing in brick joints of any brickwork helps to make water run off the wall, rather than soaking into the bricks.

Track

Track maintenance gangs were those lazy people leaning on their shovels you saw when you were going past their worksite; however the reason they were idle was because their worksite was covered by your train, and, sensibly, they were standing to one side, rather than being hit by the train.

Their job was to keep the track in alignment so that trains could run safely at full speed. Members of the track maintenance staff would carry out the patrolling of the tracks looking for defects and reporting on them, as well as looking for defects in fencing, earth slopes and anything else that might affect the safe running of the railway. Any defects found would be reported to the ganger and escalated up to the local inspector or engineer if the work was outside that which could be done by the local gang.

Many railways issued the gangers with a calendar detailing the routine work that was to be carried out in a particular week. These tasks were generally seasonal, such as taking off and oiling the fishplates connecting the rails in late spring to allow for expansion of the rails, grass-cutting and ditch cleaning.

Each gang would be protected by a lookoutman, who was equipped with a whistle (or horn) and flags. As the name suggests, his duty was to watch for approaching trains and warn the gang in time for them to get clear by blowing the whistle or horn. The man in charge was responsible for appointing a lookoutman or men.

In the 21st century, most of the work is done at night, when trains are not running. Much of the work has been mechanised, with the track alignment being carried out by computerised railway machinery. (The big yellow vehicles seen during daytime stabled in sidings as you go past).

In the 19th century much of the track renewal work was carried out between trains. The 1860s accident at Staplehurst in Kent was caused by this type of working. A passenger in the train involved was Charles Dickens. At Staplehurst, the gang had taken out part of the track without properly checking in the traffic notices if a train was due. The ganger had misread the timetable for the trains connecting with the cross-channel boats. The time at which the trains ran varied day by day according to the tides at Dover.

Gradually more and more work was carried out with the lines closed. In the early days everything was done by hand (it takes 20 men to lift a 60ft long rail), doing a quarter mile in around eight hours with the ballast being laid the next weekend, and trains going slowly over the affected area. Over the years more and more machinery has been introduced leading to the highly sophisticated machines used today which can completely relay a quarter mile of track in 6 hours, with all the ballasting done and consolidated, so that trains can run at normal speed immediately following the work.

Buildings

With all railway buildings, the maintenance is the same as is required for a house, but on a larger scale. The trades used were bricklayers, carpenters, stone masons, plumbers, roofers, plasterers and painters.

Signalling

The signalling required regular attention to replace broken wires and rodding connecting the signal box to the signals and points, as well as attending to all the equipment mounted in the ground floor of the old style mechanical signal boxes. There would be racks of mechanical interlocking that prevented signals being cleared for conflicting train movements, all of which required cleaning and lubricating.

The first electrical signalling installations on a substantial scale were made around 1926, and the area of control was no longer limited to the length of rodding that the signalman could pull for switching trains between tracks. From the 1960s the growth of electronics has enabled to control areas to be vastly increased. Instead of a signal box on average every mile, the nearly 400 miles between London (Kings Cross) and Edinburgh are controlled by 8 signal centres.

Some of the books written by former signalmen show pictures of the box interiors, together with references to the maintenance work carried out by the signal linesmen and fitters.

Telecommunications

As with buildings, much of the work was identical to that done outside the railway, with the maintenance staff being trained in the electrical requirements of the telegraph and telephone systems, both within the buildings and outside in cable runs and the long runs of wires on poles which used to parallel every railway line in the country.

CHAPTER FIVE
Maintaining the Trains

Maintenance was carried out at many places across the country. Day to day inspection and minor repairs would tend to be carried out at a workshop or depot, or even in the open air.

Most locomotives would return to their allocated shed once every 24 hours for refuelling with coal and for cleaning of the firebox and ashpan. Water had to be taken on every few hours and could be done at a station or goods yard. On a weekly basis the boiler would be drained and examined and refilled before a fire was lit. In the 20th century, express passenger locomotives (except on the Southern Railway and its constituents) were fitted with scoops to collect water from troughs sited between the rails at speed, so it was possible to make non-stop runs of between 100 and 300 miles. Drivers were expected to check their locomotive for defects, repair any minor items, and oil all bearings, reporting any more serious defects found to the staff at the shed.

In the shed, there would be facilities for changing wheel sets and the white-metal bearings, as well as minor boiler repairs and cleaning. Some of the larger sheds were capable of carrying out (and staffed to do) fairly

major repairs nearly up to the level carried out in a main works and were provided with the necessary jacks and overhead cranes to enable them to lift a locomotive off its wheels.

Some work for passenger coaches could be carried out in the carriage sheds in the vicinity of major stations, and likewise wagon repairs would be undertaken at the major goods and shunting yards around the country, often in the open air, and in all weathers.

Major repairs necessitated the vehicles being returned to a works, such as those listed above under Construction. All these works carried out major repairs, repainting and refurbishment. However, there were also smaller establishments where work was carried out, and these included:

Location	Locomotives	Carriages	Wagons
Earlestown			Yes
Inverness	Yes	Yes	Yes
Carlisle			Yes
New Cross Gate, London			Yes
Bricklayers Arms, London	Yes		
Stewarts Lane, London	Yes		
Wolverhampton	Yes	Yes	Yes
Saltley, Birmingham		Yes	Yes
Cowlairs, Glasgow	Yes	Yes	Yes
St Rollox, Glasgow	Yes	Yes	Yes
Bow, London	Yes		

The variety of trades represented in a major works would be enormous. The works would have a foundry, coppersmiths, blacksmiths with ironworking forges, and steam hammers, turners with their lathes, boiler makers, crane drivers along with a mass of labourers. A foundry would require pattern-makers and moulders; the patternmakers would make the patterns for items to be cast in brass, iron or steel, after making due allowance for the shrinkage of the molten metal, and the moulders would pack sand around the pattern in moulding boxes, before men tapped the furnace to draw off the molten metal and pour it into the moulds.

CHAPTER SIX
Operating the Railway

The departments that were involved in operating the railway were many and had a variety of titles. The exact titles and work responsibilities varied greatly, and were particularly governed by the size of the company. At the head of the tree would be the General Manager, who was responsible to the Board of Directors for everything that went on within the Company. Under his direct control would be the Secretary, whose department handled all the company business and general correspondence, with a mass of clerks. There would also be a Solicitor for all the legal affairs that arise from a business (in the smaller companies, perhaps a local lawyer would be appointed as the Railway's Solicitor).

The other Chief Officers reporting to the Board through the General Manager could include any or all of the following. The exact titles varied from company to company:

◆ **Superintendent of the Line** (or **Traffic Manager**). His department organised the timetabling of trains (both passenger and freight), the staffing of stations, the signalmen controlling the trains, and, in some cases, was the manager for the drivers and firemen. The department oversaw the work of the Station Masters (and Goods' Agents if there was no Goods' Manager).

Staff records may be found under departments such as Traffic or Coaching, which were passenger sub-sections of the Superintendent of the Line. The Goods side may have sections such as Goods, Parcels or Commercial.

- **Engineer** or **Chief Engineer** (Resident Engineer in the case of the London & South Western Railway). Responsible for the inspection and upkeep of all the earthworks, track, bridges and buildings.

- **Goods' Manager**. Responsible for the running of all the goods yards and the handling of goods between the railway and its customers by means of a large fleet of horse drawn carts.

- **Locomotive, Carriage and Wagon Superintendent** (sometimes **Chief Mechanical Engineer**). Responsible for the design and ordering of new trains for construction in the railway's own works or by contractors. Also arranged for repairs and renovation of the rolling stock owned by the company. In some instances he was the manager who controlled the drivers and firemen as part of his functions.

- **Locomotive Running Superintendent**. Responsible for providing the locomotives and staffing them. Came under the Locomotive, Carriage and Wagon Superintendent, Chief Mechanical Engineer or the Superintendent of Line.

- **Electrical Engineer**. Responsible for the distribution of electricity around the railway, and for the provision of electric trains in the 20th century when the company had decided this was necessary to handle the traffic. Initially this started off as an appointment under the Engineer, but as electricity became more commonplace, it was found desirable to separate the departments.

- **Telegraph Superintendent**, later **Signal and Telecommunications Engineer**. In the early days his work was a part of the Engineer's department. As communication links and electro-magnetic relays came into use in signalling the complexity required a specialist engineer to run this part of the business.

- **Continental Traffic Manager** or **Shipping Manager**. Appointed for those railways with links across the English and Irish Channels. Responsible for the shipping fleets and connecting rail services.

- **Accountant** and **Auditor**. These people and their staff had the responsibility for keeping the accounts, and checking that all stations and depots were handling money in accordance with the laid down procedures. Audit teams would visit every station on a regular basis, but without prior warning of their visit.

Within all these departments, there would be clerks to keep the records and write the letters. In each case their work would be overseen by a Chief Clerk for the department and major stations and depots and a clerk in charge for the smaller stations down to the small country station where the Station Master was his own clerk and chief clerk.

The engineering departments would have the specialist technical staff and the draughtsmen and tracers in the drawing offices in addition to their clerical staff. The technical staff would carry out design work and organise the planning and implementation of works delegated to them, including supervision out on site to ensure that the railway's own labour or contractors carried out the work according to the specified designs and time scales.

Station Masters

A Station Master was the manager in charge of a passenger station. His responsibilities could range from a small rural station with, perhaps, half a dozen employees, to the grandeur of a main line terminal station like Edinburgh Waverley or Paddington with several hundred employees.

Any Station Master would be expected to be on-call for problems at any time of the day or night. In the event of a train accident or fatality on the line, he would be one of the first people called to the scene, and it would be his responsibility to arrange immediate attention and first aid and to inform his superiors of what had occurred and what was being done about it. Any important travellers would be greeted personally by the station master and escorted between their carriage and the train. At a station like York, where there were passenger train services running through the night, there was even a Night Station Master with his own office.

At the smaller stations he would be an active supervisor of all the activities covering both passenger and goods traffic, as well as the signalmen. Those at rural stations were generally prominent in local affairs, and were expected to encourage local businesses to send traffic by his railway rather than by using the services of any competitor. If there was no booking clerk at the station, the Station Master would undertake the accountancy duties of balancing the books for ticket issues, and would arrange to draw money from a bank to make up the wage packets for the staff under his control.

At a medium size station, where there was a substantial amount of goods and parcels traffic, a Goods' Agent would be appointed as someone of similar grade to the Station Master, and working as a colleague rather than as a subordinate.

In the major stations, like those in Manchester, London and Edinburgh, the Station Master was a superior being. He would be present to oversee the departure of the most important trains, generally wearing a top hat, certainly up to the 1930s. Of course, if royalty were travelling, the Station Master would be present along with more senior members of the railway hierarchy, up to the General Manager of the company.

For the medium size station, the Station Master would have a number of Inspectors to oversee the station duties on an hour by hour basis, along with a number of booking clerks to issue the tickets and account for all the money taken at the station. A large station might have an Assistant Station Master to assist with the management at times when the Station Master was busy or off-duty.

At a minor station, the Station Master was really a jack of all trades, and would be found assisting in the sale and collection of tickets and seeing all trains depart. He would also almost certainly have to do all the station accounting, as there might well be no clerk there to do that.

Inspectors

There would be a number of Inspectors to assist Station Masters in the day to day, not to say minute to minute, running of a station. The number would depend upon the size of the station, but a medium size station would have at least one Inspector to supervise the porters, whilst a large London terminal would have several Inspectors on duty at any time, each with his own area of responsibility, either a physical area, or a particular range of work.

The Inspectors were responsible for making sure the porters did their job properly and that there were adequate numbers of staff to handle luggage and parcels.

Where a Station Master had no assistant, and the station was open all night, there might be an Inspector appointed to work on nights overseeing the general activities on the station.

As well as the inspectors at stations and goods depots, there would be inspectors within the Locomotive Running and Engineering departments, carrying out a variety of day to day supervisory duties. These would include making visits to staff working away from a depot.

When a senior manager was going out to visit places within his control, an Inspector or two would often accompany the manager to give up to date answers to queries.

Booking Clerks

The Booking Clerk derives his title from the days of the stage coaches when the names of passengers were entered in a large ledger, and paper tickets filled in with the name and journey details issued to the passengers as authority for them to travel. This process was initially used on the railways but it became too cumbersome with the large numbers of people travelling (6 or 12 on a stage coach – 100 or more on a train). A booking clerk, named Thomas Edmondson, in the 1840s working on the Newcastle &

Carlisle Railway, invented a system whereby consecutively numbered card tickets could be extracted from a rack and given to the passenger without needing much paperwork.

These card tickets continued to be used as the normal method of ticket issuing for the next 140 years, until the 1980s when computerised ticket issuing machines came into use.

As well as issuing tickets, the Booking Clerks were responsible for all the accounting functions both for ticket issue, and for all other revenue generated at a station, except where there was a separate Goods' Agent.

In medium and small size stations the senior booking clerk would see to the making up of wage packets. At the largest stations, a clerk would be specially appointed to look after the pay and associated paperwork such as timesheets.

Porters

Porters were really the men of all trades at a station or goods depot. They would do all the loading and unloading of parcels and passenger luggage and generally assist passengers on the platforms to find their trains. They would also sweep the station platforms and clean windows and toilets on the station when not attending to passengers and trains. At stations where trains terminated, they would sweep out the carriage, clean toilets and windows, and refill water tanks on carriages. They would also attend to the oil and gas lights and switch on electric lights when these were introduced.

A good porter would have the opportunity for promotion to a supervisory grade, such as Inspector.

At small stations they would often go round the area, filling and trimming the oil lamps fitted behind signal arms to provide an indication during darkness. Larger stations would have specially appointed lampmen to attend to lamps behind the signals and on the station.

Cleaners

In a railway context, these were junior grades within the Locomotive Department, who cleaned the engines in the engine sheds. The railway grade of Cleaner was the junior grade of Engineman, and would normally work his way up to be a Fireman after gaining experience, by cleaning, of the locomotives when they were stabled in the loco shed. A very dirty job, as the duties included cleaning out the ashpan and smokebox of locomotives when they had completed a turn of duty, then cleaning all the accumulated dirt from the locomotive.

After a few years of gaining familiarity with the components of an engine, the Cleaner would be given a bit of instruction in how to stoke a fire by working on a shunting engine. If he proved competent, promotion to Passed Cleaner took place. As a Passed Cleaner, he would be called upon to act as a Fireman for duties on local trains, and after a specified number of turns of duty would be available for promotion to Fireman as and when a vacancy occurred.

Cleaner used on its own in railway records can be assumed to refer to a locomotive cleaner unless the context makes it obvious that another role was involved. There were also carriage cleaners, whose role was to sweep out the carriages and clean the windows and toilets, but they would be described as a general rule as carriage cleaners.

Firemen

This was the man who stoked the fire in a railway steam engine, and assisted the driver by keeping a lookout for signals. He had been promoted from the ranks of the cleaners and could expect eventually to be promoted to Driver, first as a Passed Fireman and then when a vacancy occurred, became a Driver. As a Fireman he would work his way up through the links (see Glossary), starting with locomotives shunting in goods yards, then to local goods trains, moving on to suburban passenger trains and ultimately faster and longer distance trains, both passenger and freight.

A Fireman would be expected to have a very good knowledge of the railway Rule Book, and especially those sections relation to the operation of trains.

Drivers

In the mind of the public, Drivers were seen as the aristocrats of the railway. The lowest Drivers in seniority would handle the shunting locomotives in yards. As their seniority increased, they took charge of local goods trains, then local passenger trains and long distance goods trains, The most senior Drivers would be in charge of locomotives hauling the fastest passenger trains. Like Firemen, they were required to know the Rule Book.

Drivers who showed ability, and supervisory skills might well be promoted to the grade of Locomotive Inspector, with the role of overseeing the professional competency of Drivers, Firemen and Cleaners. It would be a Locomotive Inspector who examined Cleaners for promotion to Firemen, and Firemen for promotion to Drivers.

Guards

A Guard was responsible for the timekeeping of the trains on which he rode, and would keep a journal showing the times at which the train passed stations and other key places. If the train was delayed, management would call for his journal, and this would be used in apportioning blame. The person selected for blame would be asked to explain. In railway jargon the request for a report would often be referred to as a 'Please Explain' as these were the opening words, and when on a printed form were followed by lines on which could be hand-written the reason for the request.

Some guards were classified as Goods Guards or Passenger Guards, according to the type of train that they worked. On some railways there were Ballast Guards who worked the trains required by the Engineering departments. Certainly up to the 1970s there were a number of Ballast Guards working in Southern England.

Company Housing

To attract staff, many companies provided terraces of houses to accommodate their staff, with notable examples being at Crewe, Swindon and Ashford (Kent) where complete new towns were built with shops and, of course, a church; foremen and managers would have more palatial houses befitting their higher status.

Not only the major works had company housing, but even some remote stations had a terrace or two of railway houses. Tebay on the East side of the Lake District on the main line between Lancaster and Carlisle is a case in point. There was a need for additional locomotives to be attached to trains to provide extra power for the climb to Shap summit, so the Lancaster & Carlisle Railway established an engine shed at this remote collection of a few houses. The engine crews needed accommodation, and the only practicable solution was to provide a terrace of houses next to the station for them and the track maintenance staff.

A Station Master would have accommodation within the station buildings (except for very large urban stations) and was expected to attend incidents affecting the railway 24 hours a day in return for a low rent.

A crossing keeper might have a company house adjacent to the crossing, so that they could be available at all times. Opening and closing the gates might be a 'family' business with husband and wife sharing the duties. Along the South Coast between Brighton and Portsmouth and elsewhere around the country, the crossing houses still stand, although now crossing keepers are a rarity, with increasing remote control using television monitors viewed at the controlling signal box.

Communications

One essential for a widespread industry is good communications and the railway has been at the forefront of telegraph, telephone, teleprinter, and now e-mail as a medium of quick and accurate transmission of the essential information regarding the movement of trains.

In the early days, the only method available was the telegraph instrument, with its needles and clicking noise and the human operator at the receiving end had to note down the letters one by one as the transmitting operator worked the instruments. The telegraph was invented by Cooke and Wheatstone before 1837, and used zinc/acid battery power. The London & Birmingham Railway was the first to install the telegraph system. The Great Western Railway followed and had it in place by 1840.

Messages had to be written down and then passed to the person addressed, requiring staff to transcribe the flicking needles. Messengers, often young boys, then distributed the telegraph messages.

Come the 20th century, and the telephone began to be installed. Again the railway was one of the earliest industries to use it. There were two main functions – one to enable outsiders to contact the railway. Secondly for internal communication between offices. The first switchboards were manually operated with plugs to make the connections. Gradually the dial system using the rotary switch came into use for internal office systems.

Teleprinters were the next telecommunication improvement, in the 1930s, and enabled a typed message to be received. This was a major advance, enabling a true record to be available of the transmitted message, which was important when safety related messages were being transmitted like details of altered train services that had to be sent to every signal box and station along the route. Teleprinters have evolved into the modern Telex.

Staff were employed in the major stations and depots to work the telegraph and teleprinter machines, whist at smaller stations there would always be a member of staff available who could send and receive messages. Messengers would be used to distribute the received messages to the intended recipient.

As late as the 1960s, the railway telephone network relied on operators to connect one between exchanges. Dial telephones were only used within the administrative offices. When I was at Brighton in 1964, it was possible to dial within the station area, but to contact the Regional HQ in London or our outside staff required the services of the Brighton switchboard operator.

Gradually trunk dialling was introduced superseding the manned switchboards. Today the railway has a network of telephone connections that is nationwide without going outside the railway system. Even today on the railway, one occasionally hears or sees reference being made to the 'National Telephone' or to the 'Internal Phone'.

CHAPTER SEVEN
Commercial Activity

Whilst all railway activity could be considered to be commercial, the practice has been to segregate, in the staff registers, the staff primarily involved with running the trains from those whose activities did not take them onto the tracks.

In many cases, the work was carried out by contractors, depending upon the policy of the railway company concerned. For example the South Eastern Railway did not have any restaurant cars of its own, but facilities were provided by the Pullman Car Company on certain trains at a premium fare. The staff on the Pullman Cars were employed by the Pullman Car Company.

Freight

Goods trains have been a part of the railway scene from the very first public railways. In fact transport of freight was the primary reason for the construction of the plateways and the first railway wagons.

When the public railways, such as the Stockton & Darlington in 1825 started, the main purpose was really to carry coal from the coalfields to ports and then by sea to the major cities.

As the railway system expanded, so did the variety and quantity of freight carried in wagons grew. The railways would provide wagons for the transport of almost everything. It was possible to load a wagon at one end of the country, and have the railways transport goods hundreds of miles.

A specialist side of the Freight department was the conveyance of coal from the coal mines to the thousands of small goods yards around the country where coal merchants would unload the wagons onto stock piles of the various types of coal, and then bag it up into one hundredweight sacks for delivery to their customers.

Other bulk commodities handled were bricks, salt, stone and iron ore, as well as the seasonal traffics such as sugar beet and broccoli. A special traffic was the transport of bananas in heated vans; as soon as a ship berthed the bananas were loaded straight into the vans, and the train was run at fast speed to its destination.

In recent years the term 'Goods Train' has fallen out of use, and been replaced by 'Freight Train'. Interestingly, the Working Timetables used by staff have used the term Freight since 1948 or earlier.

The railway carries a considerable amount of traffic for its own purposes in maintaining the infrastructure. Because of the predominant material carried these trains are referred to as 'Ballast Trains', even when they are carrying no ballast.

Parcels

There was a great demand for the railways to carry parcels, both those that were being carried by passengers and also for unaccompanied packages from place to place. Gradually, the use of the facility grew, and one could hand in a parcel at the local station and it would be delivered to a distant station and then forwarded by the railway's own cartage service to the recipient address. This even extended to full wagon loads of parcels. The individual packets were handled on and off the trains by the parcels staff at stations.

Depending on the volume of traffic, the start of the journey could be by local train travelling in the guard's van loaded by the local station staff, and then transhipped at a junction onto another train, and so on until the packet reached the final station and was collected by or delivered to the recipient.

In cities like London, there were separate parcels depots, like Bricklayers Arms on the South Eastern Railway or Somers Town on the Midland Railway where the cartage teams would go round and collect all the parcels, deliver them to the depot, where teams of men would load all the parcels for, say, Sheffield or Dover, into one wagon. A similar process in reverse existed for wagon loads of parcels arriving in London to be delivered to the recipient's door.

Advertising

Railways have been seen as a good place to advertise wares for sale; stations were the obvious place. The initial signs were made from enamel coated plate, but gradually painted boards and then printed posters stuck to advertising hoardings came into being.

This required staff to put up and take down signs, and the clerks to administer the rental from the outside advertisers.

The railways themselves saw opportunities to advertise their own products, such as special excursions and cheap fares to a receptive audience and so the railway posters came into existence – the classic examples are the Jolly Fisherman advertising Skegness, and the well known series of railways subjects covered by Terence Cuneo, initially for the London & North Eastern Railway and then for British Railways. Many of the posters were used to promote railway excursions and travel, and a number of board sites were set aside for the railway's own purposes, rather than commercial advertising of goods marketed by other businesses.

Ticket Printers

There were a number of places where the railway carried out printing of tickets using their own staff – Crewe, Derby, Glasgow, London (Paddington) and York certainly. There may well have been other places, as far as the major railways were concerned.

Some contractors existed who were able to carry out printing of standard card railway tickets – Williamson of Ashton under Lyne, Thomas Edmondson and Glasgow Numerical Printing are some of the companies who were involved.

Refreshment Rooms

In the days of the stagecoach, refreshment stops were made at intervals for the driver and guard, not to mention the passengers to grab a hasty meal. This custom was continued by the railways, with, for example, the trains between London to Bristol making a stop at Swindon for passengers to patronise the station refreshment rooms, operated by a contractor. Other railways followed suit at stations like Normanton just north of Sheffield. Initially contractors tendered for the operation of the rooms, but gradually the operation was transferred to the railway company itself.

Most major stations would have a refreshment room, or rather two or three, to cater for the different classes of passenger. Train passengers could often send a telegram ahead, using the railway telegraph network, to order a hamper from a refreshment room to be delivered to them at a station. All this provided work for railwaymen.

As trains speeded up and with the provision of restaurant cars, there was less need, or time, for passengers to leave the train for a meal. This resulted in the closure of the facilities at Swindon, Normanton and elsewhere.

Restaurant Cars

The Great Northern Railway first tried a dining car on a train between London (Kings Cross) and Leeds in the 1870s. This was the first time meals had been cooked on a train, and proved to be successful and popular.

More and more companies built restaurant and dining cars. These were generally used on trains running more than 100 miles, with journey times of 2 or more hours.

The cars were crewed by one or two chefs, some stewards and a supervisor, often called a Conductor, who would show passengers to their seats, take the orders and collect the money.

The early restaurant cars had no connection to other vehicles in the train, but in the 20th century through connections between coaches evolved, and it was possible for dining facilities to be available to all passengers (generally separate vehicles were provided for First and Third class passengers) and there were multiple sittings for luncheon or dinner, particularly on the Anglo-Scottish journeys which were of eight or more hours duration.

Pullman Cars

In the United States, George Mortimer Pullman pioneered the construction and operation of sleeping and dining carriages. Pullman was an early entrepreneur, and decided that Europe was a good territory into which he could expand.

A number of British railways, starting with the Midland Railway in 1874, entered into agreement with Pullman, by which he would provide sleeping and dining carriages on their principal trains. Pullman would staff the vehicles, making appropriate charges to passengers using his services.

The London Brighton & South Coast Railway engaged the Pullman Car Company to provide a high class service between London (Victoria) and Brighton, known as the 'Southern Belle'. This evolved in 1933 into the all-electric 'Brighton Belle'.

Along with the 'Brighton Belle' many trains conveyed a single Pullman car in Kent and Sussex. Travel in the Pullman cars attracted a premium payment over and above the standard fare for the journey. In 1964, I was living in digs working in Brighton, but needed to come to London for my technical training on a Tuesday. I would leave the office at 5 pm on a Monday, walk down onto the station, and get the 5.15 Brighton Belle up to Victoria for a supplement of 1s.6d (7½ pence). The best bit was that I could get a hot, inexpensive snack on the train served at my seat. The ultimate in Pullman style was provided by the Blue Pullman trains between London and Bristol, Swansea or Manchester providing high speed luxury travel.

The Pullman Car Company based at Brighton built and repaired its own coaches and had a large workforce of chefs, stewards and conductors, who were located at bases around the country.

Buffet Cars

Buffet cars, as we know them, are a recent innovation. The first buffet cars started to be operated by the Big Four railways in the late 1920s, with staff from the railway restaurant car service. On the Southern Railway, most of the staff came from the Pullman Car Company.

Sleeping Cars

Sleeping cars started to be operated for overnight journeys in 1873, initially between London and Scotland. The first cars were little more than ordinary compartment style vehicles with two or four berths per compartment, and just a blanket or two. Over time, new trains were built and first class became single or twin berth per compartment and third class with four berths. Better and more linen and washing facilities were provided.

Each car, or pair of cars, was staffed by an attendant. Passengers would be woken, with a cup of tea and biscuits, in time to get off at their destination.

As well as the Anglo-Scottish services, there were sleeping cars from London to Holyhead, Leeds, Plymouth and Penzance, with cross country services from Plymouth to Newcastle, and Birmingham to Edinburgh. East Anglia and the South East were the only areas not served by sleeping cars.

Hotels

Among the first hotel chains were those operated by the railway companies. A market was seen for providing accommodation close to railway stations in key towns, cities and ports around the country as the number of commercial travellers rose and more businessmen need accommodation.

Places such as Edinburgh, Inverness, Glasgow, York, Newcastle, Derby, Liverpool, Hull, Manchester, Birmingham and London all had railway hotels located on stations. A secondary market arose for the leisure industry, and it was for this that hotels such as the Tregenna Castle at St Ives and Gleneagles, with its golf course, were developed.

As a result, included in the railway staff would be all the trades associated with the management and running of major hotels.

Laundries

For those companies that operated hotels. refreshment rooms, restaurant cars and sleeping cars, a need existed for laundering all the linen used. Probably, initially, this was contracted out to small, local, companies or groups of washerwomen, but gradually the work was taken 'in house' and the railways established laundries. By the 1950s this work was undertaken at a large central laundry serving the whole country at Willesden in North West London. The date of commencement of this by the railway is not known to the author.

Harbours and docks

Railways which served coastal areas gradually realised that there was a commercial advantage in having their own facilities for transferring goods and passengers from rail to ship. For the routes to Ireland and Europe, a number of railway-owned and operated harbours and piers were constructed. Examples are: Stranraer, Heysham, Holyhead, Fishguard, Weymouth, Lymington (Hants), Southampton, Newhaven, Folkestone, Harwich, Immingham and Grimsby along with Fishbourne, Yarmouth and Ryde on the Isle of Wight). As well, there were places like Plymouth, Portsmouth and Dover where the railway had substantial installations alongside those of other organisations or port authorities.

With the ownership of the harbours, came the maintenance responsibilities. At Newhaven and Holyhead, if not elsewhere, there was a labour force to carry out all the repairs to jetties, under the control of a Resident Engineer. So you could well find carpenters, divers, blacksmiths, riveters, crane drivers, bricklayers and masons at the port as well as those people associated with handling the ships from the shore and the loading and unloading of passengers and goods.

There were many locations around the coast where a railway branch served a pier or small quay, but where the railway only provided transport to and from the edge of the water for passengers and goods.

Ships

The following railway companies operated shipping themselves:

- London Brighton & South Coast Railway (Newhaven – Dieppe and Portsmouth – Ryde (IOW))

- London & South Western Railway (Portsmouth – Ryde (IOW), Lymington – Yarmouth (IOW), and Weymouth – Channel Islands)

- Great Western Railway (Weymouth – Channel Islands, Fishguard – Rosslare). There were also tenders at Plymouth, which transferred passengers and their luggage to and from the ocean going liners which called at Plymouth but were too large for the port installations.

- Great Eastern Railway (Harwich – Hook of Holland)

- South Eastern & London Chatham & Dover Joint Managing Committee (Dover/Folkestone to Calais/Boulogne)

- Manchester, Sheffield & Lincolnshire Railway (later Great Central Railway) – from Grimsby and the Humber ferry from New Holland to Hull

- Furness Railway (Lake Windermere services)

- North British Railway (Loch Lomond and on the Clyde)

- Caledonian Railway (Clyde services)

The 1923 grouping into the Big Four reduced the number of companies involved. During both World Wars most of the ships owned by the railway companies were 'called to the colours'. Some 200 ships in all served as troop carriers, hospital ships, minesweepers and seaplane carriers. A number of ships were lost on active service.

Buses

A number of companies operated buses to serve areas where no railway line had been built. In almost all cases the services operated from a railhead to outlying towns and villages. The Great Western Railway had a substantial network of routes in the West Country.

There were bus drivers and conductors employed, along with motor bus mechanics and fitters.

The first services started around 1903, and were sold off to major bus operators in the first few years of the 1930s.

Some experiments were carried out in the 1930s with bus type vehicles which also had a set of railway wheels, so that the vehicle could start off in a town centre, drive along the road to a station and using a specially prepared surface between and beside the rails, could lower its rail wheels and run as a train to a junction station.

CHAPTER EIGHT
Fire, Police, Ambulance

In the days before centralisation of emergency response, the railways took precautions to protect their property as they had available to them numbers of disciplined staff who could be trained for certain emergency response duties.

Railway Police

The Railway Policeman started as a general purpose 'man about the station' to help the passengers, watch out for thieves and a signaller of trains. By the end of the 1840s the role of signalling the trains was passed on to dedicated signalmen in signal boxes or cabins and the policemen became law enforcement officers. Gradually the Railway Police evolved from officers employed by individual companies and limited to that company's territory, into today's national British Transport Police. Formed after nationalisation in 1948, the British Transport Police are responsible for all the usual police duties, but, uniquely, have become a unified force available to deal with crime and emergencies anywhere on the railway network. This was well illustrated after the July 2007 bombing in London, when at Waterloo and Charing Cross there were officers from Wales patrolling the stations.

At almost every major train accident, some of the police presence would be provided by the railway company's own police officers, but with the assistance of the local civil police, who would generally be on the scene before the railway police.

For records of the Railway Police forces, I suggest that the TNA Research Guide on Transport Police will provide helpful information.

Fire Brigade

If you look at pictures of railway stations and signalboxes, especially pre 1930, in a prominent position there would be a number of red painted fire buckets. These would be kept clean and filled with water or, in some cases, sand, to provide an immediate firefighting tool. These would enable the local staff to deal with minor fires quickly before they could spread. In the cases of grass fires ignited by sparks from locomotives the local track maintenance gangs would attend with beaters to put the fire out.

With only rudimentary fire brigades other than in large towns, it was an essential business protection for the railway to be able to extinguish fires on their property quickly before much damage and disruption had occurred.

In the big workshops, there were often men detailed to attend fires in the works complex, using equipment kept for the purpose. In a few cases, like Crewe and Swindon, there would be a Fire Brigade who would have a big shiny fire engine of a similar type to the local civil fire brigade, but probably purchased second-hand.

Fire fighting competitions

As an incentive to improve the staff skills at firefighting, many railway companies instituted annual competitions, with a shield awarded to the winner. Stations and depots would form teams that would vie with their rivals to see who was the most efficient. The winners would hold the shield for a year; some of the shields would have tens of plaques listing the winning teams.

Fire Trains

During the two World Wars, small locomotives and tank wagons were coupled into trains to go anywhere on the railway network to extinguish fires. The locomotive was fitted with a steam-driven pump and hoses. What use was actually made of the trains to handle real fires is not clear. My suspicion is that it was only in cities in the Second World War where there were conflagrations (e.g. Plymouth and

Portsmouth city centres) that the fire trains have been called out, principally to protect railway property.

Ambulance

Gradually the railway industry took more responsibility for the welfare of its staff. At the major locations there would be an ambulance room to attend to staff who had been injured, and they might even treat members of the public who had been injured on the railway. As time went on, the facilities and staff grew, and several of the London terminals had a first aid room staffed by a nurse.

There was also the need to check staff medically, to ensure they were fit to carry out their duties in a safe manner. Initially, this would be done by a local doctor by arrangement with the railway, but, gradually, doctors were employed to do the necessary checks. One of the key tests carried out was for colour vision, in view of the necessity of staff being able to distinguish the various signal colours by day and by night. The doctors would also advise managers on safety and safety issues.

I can recall a query being raised in the early days of diesel locomotives about staff inhaling the fumes from the exhausts when working in tunnels. The answer was that the fumes were not injurious to health; surprising as one finished a shift with eyes watering and a sore throat!

St John and St Andrew's Ambulance Associations

I do not know exactly when the voluntary ambulance work on the railway started, but it was in full swing in the early part of the 20th century. Due to the isolated nature of much railway work, staff were encouraged to undertake training in basic first aid. This was done through the auspices of the St John and St Andrew's Ambulance Associations. Staff would attend, in their own time, one evening a fortnight, with classes being run every week to allow for the shift working. The classes would be taken by a local doctor or qualified first aiders working to the Ambulance Association training handbook.

There was an incentive to pass, as many companies would grant an extra day of leave each year to those who had achieved the standard and, in some cases, a free ticket in recognition of the time put in. Staff had to requalify at intervals, and there were local and national competitions, especially for teams from the major works like Swindon, and stations like Edinburgh Waverley. The results of the competitions for teams and individuals were reported in the staff magazines. Like the firefighting competitions, the winner would hold a shield for a year before passing it on to the best team for the next year.

The staff who had qualified, and they were many, rendered the immediate first aid in what is one of the more dangerous industries. Undoubtedly, they lessened the effect of injuries and saved many lives. When there were major accidents, frequently the trained railway first aid staff would be first on the scene, well before any ambulance or medical people.

A number of senior managers held high rank within the Ambulance Associations.

Ambulance Trains

Sometimes you will find reference to 'ambulance trains'. These were not really a railway responsibility except when it came to moving them around the system. An ambulance train was a set of about a dozen coaches, converted into wards and staffed by Army medical teams, with a locomotive provided by the railway attached. The trains would be sent to the Channel Ports, generally Folkestone, Dover or Newhaven, to meet ships coming across from France with evacuated army personnel who had been wounded on the continent. The troops would be taken to military hospitals at Netley, Aldershot, Sidcup, Orpington and elsewhere.

There were trains assigned to the Navy for moving naval casualties from ports like Invergordon to naval hospitals during the First World War.

There were some trains of British coaches that went across to France by train ferry in both World Wars to assist in moving casualties from behind the front line to ports such as Calais, Dieppe and Boulogne. As in Britain, the trains were staffed by military personnel, although the drivers, firemen and train guards may well have been railwaymen who had joined the army.

CHAPTER NINE
Accidents

It might be expected that accident reports would be a fruitful source of genealogical information as the railway industry was one of the most dangerous after coal mining and quarrying.

Unfortunately for the family historian, the official reports that give names only cover the major train accidents. The overwhelming majority of staff injuries and deaths only feature as statistics in the Annual Reports by the Railway Inspectorate.

A more fruitful source of information will be local newspapers if you have the date and place, but even then the details about the people may be, at best, sketchy.

A possible clue to a railway employee having been involved in an accident would be where they were moved into a less physically arduous role. Possible examples are:

- a Signaller who became a Booking Lad, as a result of a back injury.
- a man becoming a messenger in the departmental offices after losing an arm or a eye.

There has always been a tradition of keeping staff employed, albeit on lighter duties, following industrial accidents or chronic sickness.

Some railway company files with information on general minor accidents may have survived within the RAIL series of records at TNA. The papers might be included within reports by Station Masters and the like, so there may be a mention in committee minute books.

CHAPTER TEN
Pension Funds and Trade Unions

Medical Society

Before the advent of the state-run National Health Service, staff clubbed together and contributed a small weekly sum for the men and their families to see the services of a doctor. These societies and clubs were not run by the railway and records are unlikely to have survived.

Mutual Assistance Funds

In Victorian times, a man who was laid off through ill-health was without pay, so some railway companies established funds to which the employees contributed to provide some financial support to sick and injured staff.

Generally there were a number of trustees of these funds, some elected by the staff themselves and the others being senior officials of the railway company. The Great Western Railway appointed trustees included the Chairman of the Directors and the General Manager or Chief Mechanical Engineer. The funds were invested in reputable shares such as government stocks, or in the case of the GWR, shares of the GWR itself.

Pensions

Railway companies have always been forthcoming with gratuities to long serving staff, but any such gratuity was at the discretion of the Directors. The lack of formal pension arrangements led to the formation of the Mutual Assistance Funds. After the Grouping in 1923, pension funds were set up to which the staff contributed. Initially the funds were only open to salaried staff, but gradually the wages grades were able to join funds created for them.

Trade Unions

In common with most Victorian businesses, the idea of the workforce uniting and pressing demands was anathema. Eventually the workforce combined to set up trade unions of which there were a number, each representing a particular group of staff. The earliest unions started in the 1860s, when the Engine Drivers and Firemans United Society fought for a minimum wage. The unions really came to the fore after a number of major, national, strikes, notably in 1919 and the General Strike of 1926.

The principal trade unions were:

♦ Amalgamated Society of Railway Servants (ASRS) amalgamated with United Pointsmens' and Signalmens' Society (UPSS) and General Railway Workers 'Union (GRWU) to become (in 1913) the National Union of Railwaymen which, in turn, became the National Union of Rail, Maritime and Transport Workers (RMT) in 1990.

♦ Railway Clerks' Association (formed 1897) became the Transport Salaried Staffs Association (TSSA) in 1951.

♦ Engine Drivers' and Firemen's United Society founded by 1867 – became the Associated Society of Locomotive Engineers and Firemen (ASLEF) in 1880.

There were other unions, such as the Amalgamated Engineering Union, with, as far as the railways were concerned, small numbers of members, particularly in the workshops.

The unions generally had benevolent funds to assist their members who had to retire as a result of injury or ill health in the days before any state welfare benefits. These funds were generated from part of the weekly subscription which was collected on pay day by union representatives.

Any records that survive, other than those mentioned by Tom Richards in his book, are likely to be at the University of Warwick. Local union branch records may have been deposited with local record offices or archives.

Railway Benevolent Fund

The Railway Benevolent Fund initially was established in 1858 to assist railway officers and their dependents. It rapidly expanded to assist all grades of staff and their widows and orphans.

The RBF established an orphanage at Derby (St Christopher's) mainly for the orphans of men killed in the railway service.

Orphanages

With the combination of a high fatality rate among railway employees and the relatively (to modern day thinking) early age at death, it became obvious within the railway industry that something ought to be done to look after the bereaved children.

At least one railway company founded an orphanage – the London & South Western Railway at Clapham in 1886 for orphans of staff regardless of grade. Early in the 20th century it moved to purpose built premises at Woking in Surrey. It was funded by one penny a week contributions by the railwaymen themselves with some grants from the Company Board, along with legacies from senior managers. Every pay-day, volunteers at each station and works would collect the subscriptions from their colleagues. The Great Western Railway had a Widows and Orphans Fund, with similar ideals.

A small annual sum was raised by collectors and dogs with a cash box strapped to their back that would patrol major stations such as Waterloo and Paddington in London. When the dogs died, some were stuffed and placed in a glass case on 'their' station to continue to raise funds. At London (Paddington) in the 1940s there was a model locomotive whose wheels, if a coin was placed in the slot, would rotate for a short time, and the takings went to the Widows and Orphans Fund.

Retirement and Convalescent Homes

In the 20th century the Orphanage at Woking expanded and provided sheltered accommodation for elderly and injured ex-railwaymen and their widows.

By 1922, there were convalescent homes at Lavenham, Southport, St Leonards-on-Sea, Dawlish as well as others in Kent, Cheshire and Yorkshire.

CHAPTER ELEVEN
Miscellaneous

Railway Mission and Chaplains

With the creation of railway towns such as Swindon and Crewe, railway companies paid for the provision of churches to give spiritual comfort to their staff.

In 1881 the Railway Mission was founded to provide spiritual guidance for railwaymen who were unable to attend church due to Sunday work, and irregular working hours. By 1922, 300 branches of the Mission had been established. This has continued until the present day, although the clergy concerned have never been railway staff, despite having rooms made available at stations, and access to see staff who needed their help. The Railway Mission established Convalescent Homes at St Leonards-on-Sea and Southport.

Branches of the Mission were established in South Africa and Japan. The Mission was inter-denominational.

Newspaper trains

As the newspaper industry began to cater to the mass market, the railways began to provide express trains running from London and Manchester to convey newspapers in bulk around the country. These trains supplemented dedicated parcels vans attached to overnight trains, by enabling newspaper staff to bundle up together copies of various titles for transfer to connecting trains or road transport for delivery to every town and village newsagent.

Until the early 1970s, the daily papers for the Outer Hebrides went by the night sleeper train from Glasgow to Inverness and then on the first train to Kyle of Lochalsh where they were transferred to the MacBraynes boat to Stornoway, getting there about 4 pm. In this case the papers were bundled up by the newspaper wholesalers in the vans while going from Glasgow to Inverness, and then handled by railway staff at Inverness and Kyle of Lochalsh.

Travelling Post Office and Mail Trains

Mail has been carried by railways almost from the first as the direct successors to the stage coaches. The first on-train sorting carriage dates from 1838 and was staffed by sorters from the General Post Office, and ran on the London & Birmingham Railway. From that small beginning, a network of Postal trains spread out across the country. They were called Travelling Post Offices (TPO) and in most cases there was a letter box into which the public could post letters at an enhanced fee.

The most famous of these trains was the Down Special TPO from Euston to Glasgow and Aberdeen, which was the subject of a classic documentary 'The Night Mail'. This showed the work of the Post Office staff sorting mail on the move and despatching and receiving while on the move at various points along the line. This was produced by the GPO Film Unit, and is still available in DVD format.

As well as the sorting trains, there were many mail trains which were loaded and unloaded by Post Office staff. These were supplemented by ordinary passenger trains which would carry mail under the supervision of the guard or in separate vans attached to the passenger coaches. Much of the mail carried by ordinary passenger trains was loaded and unloaded by Post Office staff rather than railway staff.

The only railway staff involvement with the postal trains like the TPOs was to run the trains, as Drivers, Firemen and Guards and to control the movement as Signallers. The postal staff on the trains were employed by the General Post Office.

Funeral Trains

An unusual operation ran between London (Waterloo) and Brookwood Cemetery from 1852 to 1941. The London Necropolis Company built a station just outside Waterloo, along with hearse vans, and used the London & South Western Railway (later Southern Railway) to operate trains conveying the deceased and the mourners to their large cemetery at Brookwood. This operation has been detailed in a book published by the Oakwood Press, which gives an insight on an unusual operation.

Railway Clearing House

As the railway network developed, problems began to arise over the method of charging for traffic transferring from one company to another. Relatively simple when there were only a few railways and sparse train services, but as the network grew it speedily became apparent that a more sophisticated solution was needed, and so in 1842 the Railway Clearing House was formed and set up in offices in Drummond Street adjacent to Euston station. At its peak it employed some 2,500 clerks.

The Railway Clearing House (RCH) provided the facilities for a fair and equitable split of revenue when a train passed from one company to another, whether passenger or goods. For example, a passenger in 1900 travelling from Kings Cross to Edinburgh would pass over the lines of the Great Northern Railway to York (188 miles) then the North Eastern Railway to Berwick-upon-Tweed (140 miles) and finally the North British Railway (75 miles). Without the Railway Clearing House arrangement in all probability, it would have been necessary for the passenger to have three tickets; with the RCH, one ticket was all that was needed, and details of ticket sales at Kings Cross for northbound passengers would be passed to the RCH, and those originating at Edinburgh to come south likewise. The RCH did all the calculations and made the settlements to the respective companies.

A similar process existed for goods traffic, and the RCH employed number takers at every junction between companies to record the individual wagon and tarpaulin numbers passing through the junction or sorting sidings, and the results were forwarded to the clerks at the RCH. The clerks calculated the proportion of the charges due to each of the railways over which each wagon or tarpaulin had travelled and, to help them, had tables and maps showing exact distances from junction points to stations and between stations.

Military Railways

From about 1905 there were a number of railways operated by the Army, both as transport within military establishments and as training units. The first of the latter was the Woolmer Instructional Military Railway in Hampshire, which, in 1935 evolved into the Longmoor Military Railway running between Liss and Bordon. Longmoor served the various camps in the area, but more importantly trained army personnel in all aspects of construction, repairing and operating railways. It was foreseen that in a war, railways were the most effective means of moving men and supplies behind the front line, and that for a European war, it might be necessary to use army staff rather than rely on the local railway staff.

Most of the men and officers were attached to the Royal Engineers or subsidiary units.

There were also military railway establishments at Bicester, Melbourne (Derby), Marchwood (Hampshire), Cairn Ryan (near Stranraer) and Plymouth Dockyard.

Territorial Army

Since the start of the Territorial Army, railway staff have been active in the Territorial Army. One of my colleagues was called up to serve in Afghanistan with the Royal Logistics Corps.

Home Guard

During the Second World War, large numbers of railway men enlisted in the Home Guard and carried out their military duties after railway work. The railway units were mainly used for guarding railway installations.

Gallantry Awards

During the Second World War, two railwaymen were awarded the George Cross for their actions in attempting to save lives when the train of bombs that they were moving caught fire and exploded at Soham in Cambridgeshire.

Another railwayman was awarded the George Cross for his actions following the failure of a pipe which sent scalding steam across the engine cab at Chapel-en-le-Frith in Derbyshire in 1957.

It should be noted that a few railwaymen were awarded the Victoria Cross during the First World War, but these were for military, not railway, actions.

Most of the men awarded a VC or GC have been commemorated with locomotives being named after them.

Honours

In the 20th century, a number of awards have been made each year to railwaymen for their public services, and these are listed in the New Year and Birthday Honours lists. There are many railwaymen who have been involved as councillors and become Mayors and Lord Mayors, often initiated by their trade union activities.

Railway Inspectorate

Her Majesty's Railway Inspectorate was founded in 1840 to inspect new railways and was part of the Board of Trade from then. In 1870, they were given powers to investigate railway accidents. The Inspectorate is not part of the railway industry. The Inspecting Officers were civil servants, who were generally recruited from the ranks of retired officers from the Royal Engineers. On the formation of the Ministry of Transport and Civil Aviation, the Railway Inspectorate was transferred from the Board of Trade. From the 1990s they have been part of the Health and Safety Executive, and have been recruited from the engineering professions.

Minor staff accidents were investigated by a team of Railway Employment Inspectors, who were civilians working under the direction of the Chief Inspecting Officer.

Shareholders

In general, shareholders were not railway employees, for the simple reason that staff did not have the finances to enable them to purchase shares. Very few records of railway shareholders survive. The major surviving listing (for the Great Western Railway) is in the hands of the Society of Genealogists, and a team is currently transcribing the details. What has become apparent as the transcription progressed is that out of 175,000 shareholders fewer than 100 are obviously railway people by the occupation recorded. Most of those connected with the railway were Trustees for mutual aid and pension funds.

Best Kept Stations and Gardens

Many railway companies encouraged their staff to enhance the appearance of the stations. As an incentive, an annual competition would be held, judged by a panel of managers, with modest prizes awarded to the best station in various categories.

The categories were devised so that the small, urban station was not competing against a larger, rural station.

In a similar manner, there were competitions for the best kept garden, where points were awarded for design and maintenance of flower beds and hanging baskets.

Winning stations would display the shield (or, more recently, the framed certificate) with pride.

CHAPTER TWELVE
London Transport Railways

The underground railways in London have similarities to the Main Line railways, but with one major difference – there was no freight traffic operated by the underground network except for the Metropolitan Railway (now the Metropolitan Line of London Underground) from North West London out to Aylesbury.

The underground lines started with the Metropolitan Railway from Praed Street (now Paddington) to Farringdon in 1865. Extensions were made and the electrified tube network started with the City & South London Railway (now part of the Northern Line) and Central London Railway in the late 19th century.

In 1933, all the underground railways in London became part of the London Passenger Transport Board, which in its turn became the London Transport Executive of the British Transport Commission in 1948.

Records are primarily held by Transport for London at their headquarters with a small number of records within the RAIL classes at TNA. There is some material held by the London Metropolitan Archives.

CHAPTER THIRTEEN
Where to Look

Census

While not being a 'railway' source, this is actually one of, if not the best sources for tracing railwaymen and their movements. With census returns available from 1841 to 1901, and now 1911, it is possible to get a snapshot of the employment location of an individual.

The entry in the census enumerator's book will give the name of the individual, their age and marital status, occupation and names and ages of any family or other people in the household and, crucially, their address. By using maps, it should be possible to get an idea of the likely places of work for a railway worker. A look at the adjacent streets may well show up other railway people.

If one is lucky, the enumerator may even have defined the occupation by adding the initials of the railway company e.g. Porter (NER), which can lead you direct to any surviving staff records at the TNA or elsewhere.

All the usual warnings apply about using census indexes. Names may not have been transcribed correctly, or they may not have been correctly entered by the enumerator.

Maps

Maps are next in the list because once you know where somebody lived, it is possible to see where the nearest railway installation was, and where he or she might have been employed. Most record offices hold copies of the 25-inch series of Ordnance Survey maps for their area. Where they were published, for major towns and cities, the 50-inch series provide a more detailed view of a smaller area on each sheet.

Ordnance Survey maps will frequently show the name of the railway company alongside the line, which can help with identification.

The Alan Godfrey series of Ordnance Survey map reproductions (at a slightly reduced scale) cover many of the urban areas where engine sheds, goods depots of major works are located and will also show signal box locations, although in the majority of cases the full name is not shown, simply 'Engine Shed' or 'Railway Works'. In general, the name of the railway company will be shown alongside each line, so this can help in identification of potential employers for your ancestor.

Undoubtedly, the best atlas of railway history is the two volumes of maps compiled by Colonel M. H. Cobb. Col. Cobb has superimposed a map of all railways in England, Scotland and Wales onto the Ordnance Survey one-inch series dating from the 1970s. Dates of opening and closing together with all stations are shown, and the colour of the line indicates which of the 4 post 1923 Groups operated each line. Company names, and dates of takeover/renaming are shown.

A simplified, and cheaper, set of maps without the Ordnance Survey background maps, but based on Col. Cobb's work, are the Railways of Britain series of which the first 3 volumes have been published, out of a total of some 40 which will eventually cover the whole country.

Deposited Plans

Before any railway line could be constructed, a plan had to be drawn up for submission to Parliament, as part of the procedure for obtaining an Act of Parliament enabling the construction of a railway; the plans are referred to as the Deposited Plans. The plans showed every parcel of land that was affected by the construction and there was a list of owners and occupiers of each, numbered, parcel of land. The list was contained in the 'Book of Reference' that accompanied the plans. A copy of the plans and book of reference had to be deposited in Parliament and with the local authorities – a process that still applies today.

Copies of the Deposited Plans and Books of Reference are now held at the Parliamentary Archives at Westminster and County Record Offices. In Metropolitan areas, the County copy may be located in the archives for the area.

The Plans and Books are of absolutely no use for tracing people who worked on the railway, but can be of considerable help if you had an ancestor who owned, or lived in a property, affected by the construction of a railway.

To make use of the plans and books for finding ancestors, it is essential that the researcher has an address and knows which railway company created the documents.

CAUTIONARY NOTE: The Act of Parliament generally was approved some two to six years before the first trains ran over the line, and the associated Plans and Books had to be submitted to parliament in advance. The parliamentary process started at least 6 months to a year before the Act for the railway was passed. For example the act for the Construction of the Canterbury & Whitstable Railway was passed in 1825, but the railway did not start operating until 1830.

The National Archives (TNA)

TNA are the place to look for the official records, such as Directors' Minutes and Staff Records. The Directors' Minutes are in the RAIL series for the particular railway, and the TNA catalogue should be consulted .For details of holdings of staff records see Tom Richards' book *Was Your Grandfather a Railwayman?* and David Hawkins' book *Railway Ancestors*.

If you are looking for items that are not directly staff records, e.g. Minute Books and files, it may be worth reading through the class lists rather than using the catalogue. By doing this your eye may be caught by something which has been missed on a computer search.

Scottish Archives

The staff records, as well as other official records, for Scottish Railways are housed in Edinburgh and the holdings are listed in Tom Richards' book *Was Your Grandfather a Railwayman?*.

County Record Offices and Local Archives

Although few County Record Offices and Local Archives have substantial collections of staff records, a certain number of records for local railways within the area may exist, and it may well be rewarding to consult the catalogue for anything relevant to your research. Known holdings are listed in Tom Richards' book *Was Your Grandfather a Railwayman?*.

Many record offices have photographic collections and it is possible that some photographs show stations or groups of staff.

There will also be maps and local histories available in many archives, and these can be of considerable use in providing background information.

I was fortunate when researching the Wainscott family to find a group photograph of the men from the Sheffield area St John Ambulance, who were going to the Boer War.

National Railway Museum

This is the repository for much general railway historical material, but has no staff records as such. From perusal of some material in the library, there are many passing references, but little is indexed by names of individuals. The staff in the Library are well informed, archival staff, and may be able to assist the researcher. Because of the nature of their archives, the staff can become relatively expert on railway records that they hold, unlike local record offices where staff may not have in depth knowledge of railways.

A select collection of books is available on the open shelves. There is also a collection of photographs which may have something relevant to your research. The cover illustration for this book came from the photographic collection.

Railway Museums and Heritage Railways

These locations may have small museums with information about local railways and with volunteers who may have expert knowledge of the particular railway that is the focus of interest. Even where the volunteers on duty have no knowledge themselves, they may know the right person to whom your enquiry should be directed.

The quantity and quality of each mini-archive depends on the interest and enthusiasm of the individual in charge.

Some, such as the Ffestiniog Railway at Porthmadog in North Wales have a considerable archive of material relating to their own railway. The people that run these railways and the associated museums are generally volunteers and work on a part-time basis, so may not be able to give an immediate response to an enquiry.

Railtrack, Network Rail and Train Operating Companies

These organisations which run the modern day railway infrastructure and train services have no staff records that can be accessed. Basically with the advent of data protection legislation, everybody within the records currently held would be protected by the Act. Similar constraints apply to the information held by current pension fund management.

Network Rail has some archive material relating to the structures and track, but does not do any research other than that needed for its own operational needs. Having over the years seen much of this material in connection with his work, the author can personally vouch that there is absolutely no material likely to be of use to the family historian. A possible exception would be for someone who had a specific interest in writing an engineering biography of a very senior civil engineer as some drawings survive, generally in microfilmed format, with signatures on the drawings signed as part of the contract documentation.

In the first instance, written approach should be made to Network Rail Community Relations staff. However it must be emphasised that individuals wishing to carry out research are rarely granted access to material and in all cases have to show extremely good grounds for needing access; a few people have been able to use records when writing books on railway or engineering history, but every case is looked at on an individual basis and access is dependent on the workload of the record keepers. The primary role of the record keepers is to supply information for the operational needs of the railway.

Newspapers

For descriptions of train accidents and staff injuries, local newspapers can be a good source, but to use them, a reasonably precise date has to be known. Without a date, much searching through the pages of small print will be needed.

Copies can be found at the British Library (Newspaper Section) or in local libraries. Increasingly, some newspapers are being digitised and this makes searching easier. The most notable example of this is *The Times*, with the digital version being fully searchable on line; this is a pay to use site, although many major public libraries have it available for their patrons.

The Times would not necessarily mention minor incidents, and a local newspaper would have to be consulted. Local papers for the area would be more likely to provide fuller details of incidents, especially names.

Local papers may have reports of a Station Master or a long serving member of staff on their retirement, especially if the individual had been prominent in local affairs outside the railway.

Railway histories

Many histories have been written about railways. However, it has to be said that few of them are relevant directly to family history, as the only persons mentioned, as a general rule, are the most senior engineers who designed the railway and the General Manager of the company. That said, the histories are a good source of background information about the railway.

Unfortunately, many railway histories written by railway enthusiasts since 1950 emphasise the locomotives and train performance rather than being a fuller history. A good list of pre-1990 works is given in *A Bibliography of Railway History* by George Ottley and others.

War Memorials

Tom Richards gives in Appendix C of *Was your Grandfather a Railwayman?*, a list of the known surviving War Memorials to Railway Staff who lost their lives serving in the two World Wars.

You may even see a modern locomotive, no 66715, owned by FirstGBRf, named 'Valour', which is a mobile war memorial; the name originated with a steam engine on the Great Central Railway, which was named in honour of railwaymen killed in World War I.

CHAPTER FOURTEEN
Case Studies of a Rail Family

The information about the various individuals has come from census returns and the staff records for the railways mentioned that are held by TNA at Kew. No references are cited, as this section is merely intended to represent the type and quantity of material that might be found. Some extra information came from material held by family members in New Zealand and has been included for completeness.

George Wainscott

George Wainscott was born in 1844 at Hereford, the son of James Wainscott, railway ticket collector on the Newport, Abergavenney and Hereford Railway at Hereford. When George married in 1864, the certificate described him as a railway servant. According to the records of the North Staffordshire Railway, he was appointed Yardman at Leek in November 1869. In April 1871, he was staying with his father in Hereford, but by the next month was living at Fenton, Stoke-on-Trent; this may have been a railway-owned house. In 1878, he was a pointsman, living at Havelock Street, Shelton. In 1881, he was living at Leek. In January 1889, he was appointed Signalman at Leek at a weekly wage of 23s.0d; every week 2s.0d was deducted for rent of a railway house. He was cautioned in

January 1902 for 'irregular signalling'. He resigned 19 April 1903. A retiring gratuity of £10 was allowed by the Directors of the company at their meeting on 21 April 1903. He died a few months later.

William Wainscott

William Wainscott was born at Leek in Staffordshire, the son of George Wainscott. An uncle of William's and at least one cousin were employed by various railways, so the Wainscotts can be said to be a 'railway' family.

William himself joined the North Staffordshire Railway in 1885, and worked in various grades at the Goods Yards at Leek and Milton, before becoming a Foreman in the yard at Milton. From the staff records, I was able to obtain details of his promotions and rates of pay. He was suspended from duty on four occasions as the result of having consumed too much alcohol. After the first and fourth of these suspensions, the records show that he took the pledge, but obviously the first time did not have much effect! He was off work injured on half-pay for two weeks in 1908. No records of pay for the 1914/18 period survive and it is possible that he was serving in the forces for that time, as there were various pay rises made during the war period. He died in 1945.

Henry Wainscott

Henry was a step brother of William Wainscott, also born at Leek (in 1879), when his father George was a Signalman. In 1898, Henry joined the Manchester, Sheffield & Lincolnshire Railway as a Clerk at Broughton Lane, Sheffield earning 20 shillings a week. (The Manchester Sheffield & Lincolnshire Railway was soon renamed the Great Central Railway in recognition of the extension from Sheffield to London (Marylebone) opened in 1900). Henry resigned in 1900, and enlisted in the St John Ambulance Brigade, in which he served as a Private and was an ambulanceman in the 5th Volunteer Detachment (Sheffield) which went to the South African War. On his return in 1902, he rejoined the Great Central Railway at Staveley, near Chesterfield. From the MS&L staff records, I learned that Henry was promoted to jobs at Leicester and Doncaster, but resigned again in August 1906 and emigrated to New Zealand. Wainscott family papers show that in December 1906, Henry joined the New Zealand Railways as a labourer. Gradually he rose through the grades, becoming a Station-master at two or more stations in the North Island. He died in 1941.

CHAPTER FIFTEEN

*Towns served by more than one
Railway Company*

The listing in the table below shows those towns where more than one company had a significant presence such as stations or engine sheds. At some of the places listed, other railways may have had a smaller presence, perhaps by exercising running powers. The listing is not exhaustive, and, in particular, does not include minor railways.

In many cities there would be agents for a number of railway companies primarily concerned with seeking goods traffic and parcels business to be routed via 'their' company.

Town	Pre-Grouping Companies	Post Grouping Companies
Aberdeen	Great North of Scotland, North British	London & North Eastern
Banbury	Great Western, Great Central, London & North Western	Great Western, London & North Eastern, London Midland & Scottish
Barnstaple	Great Western, London & South Western, Lynton & Barnstaple	Great Western, Southern
Basingstoke	Great Western, London & South Western	Great Western, Southern
Bath	Great Western, Midland, Somerset & Dorset Joint	Great Western, London Midland & Scottish
Bedford	Midland, London & North Western	London Midland & Scottish
Birmingham	Great Western, London & North Western, Midland	Great Western, London Midland & Scottish
Bodmin	Great Western, London & South Western	Great Western, Southern
Bristol	Great Western, Midland	Great Western, London Midland & Scottish
Bradford	Midland, Lancashire & Yorkshire Great Northern	London & North Eastern, London Midland & Scottish
Cambridge	Great Eastern, Great Northern, London & North Western	London & North Eastern, London Midland & Scottish
Cardiff	Great Western Barry Cardiff Taff Vale	Great Western
Carlisle	Caledonian, North Eastern, London & North Western, Furness, North British,	London Midland & Scottish, London & North Eastern

Town	Pre-Grouping Companies	Post Grouping Companies
Carlisle (*cont'd*)	Midland, Glasgow & South Western, Maryport & Carlisle	
Chester	Great Western, London & North Western, Cheshire Lines Committee	Great Western, London Midland & Scottish
Cromer	Great Eastern, Midland & Great Northern Joint	London & North Eastern
Derby	Midland, Great Northern	London & North Eastern, London Midland & Scottish
Dorchester	Great Western, London & South Western	Great Western, Southern
Dover	South Eastern, London, Chatham & Dover	Southern
Edinburgh	Caledonian, North British	London Midland & Scottish, London & North Eastern
Exeter	Great Western, London & South Western	Great Western. Southern
Glasgow	Caledonian, North British, Glasgow & South Western	London Midland & Scottish, London & North Eastern
Great Yarmouth	Great Eastern, Midland & Great Northern Joint	London & North Eastern
Guildford	South Eastern London & South Western	Southern
Hastings	South Eastern London Brighton & South Coast	Southern
Hereford	Great Western, Midland	Great Western London Midland & Scottish,
Inverness	Highland, Great North of Scotland	London Midland & Scottish, London & North Eastern
Lancaster	Midland, London & North Western	London Midland & Scottish

Town	Pre-Grouping Companies	Post Grouping Companies
Leeds	Lancashire & Yorkshire, Midland, Great Northern	London & North Eastern, London Midland & Scottish
Leicester	Great Central, Great Northern, Midland	London & North Eastern, London Midland & Scottish
Liverpool	Lancashire & Yorkshire, London & North Western, Cheshire Lines Committee, Mersey	London Midland & Scottish, London & North Eastern
London (South)	South Eastern, London Chatham & Dover, London Brighton & South Coast, London & South Western	Southern
London (West)	Great Western, Great Central	Great Western, London & North Eastern
London (East)	Great Eastern, London Tilbury & Southend	London Midland & Scottish, London & North Eastern
London (North)	London & North Western, Midland, Great Northern, North London	London Midland & Scottish, London & North Eastern
Loughborough	Great Central, Midland	London & North Eastern, London Midland & Scottish
Lowestoft	Great Eastern, Midland & Great Northern Joint	London & North Eastern
Manchester	Lancashire & Yorkshire, London & North Western, Cheshire Lines Committee	London & North Eastern, London Midland & Scottish
Morecambe	Midland, London & North Western	London Midland & Scottish
Norwich	Great Eastern, Midland & Great Northern Joint	London & North Eastern

Town	Pre-Grouping Companies	Post Grouping Companies
Nottingham	Great Central, Great Northern, Midland	London & North Eastern, London Midland & Scottish
Oxford	Great Western, London & North Western	Great Western, London Midland & Scottish
Peterborough	London & North Western, Great Northern, Great Central	London & North Eastern, London Midland & Scottish
Plymouth	Great Western, London & South Western	Great Western, Southern
Portsmouth	London & South Western, London Brighton & South Coast	Southern
Ramsgate	South Eastern London, Chatham & Dover	Southern
Reading	Great Western, South Eastern	Great Western, Southern
Rochester	South Eastern, London, Chatham & Dover	Southern
Rugby	Great Central, Midland, London & North Western	London & North Eastern, London Midland & Scottish
Salisbury	Great Western, London & South Western	Great Western, Southern
Sheffield	Manchester Sheffield & Lincolnshire/Great Central, Great Northern, Midland	London & North Eastern, London Midland & Scottish
Shrewsbury	Great Western, London & North Western	Great Western, London Midland & Scottish
Swansea	Great Western, London & North Western, Midland	Great Western, London Midland & Scottish
Templecombe	Somerset & Dorset, London & South Western	Somerset & Dorset, Southern
Winchester	Great Western, London & South Western	Great Western, Southern

Town	Pre-Grouping Companies	Post Grouping Companies
Wolverhampton	Great Western, London & North Western	Great Western, London Midland & Scottish
Yeovil	Great Western, London & South Western	Great Western, Southern
York	North Eastern, Great Northern	London & North Eastern

CHAPTER SIXTEEN
Railway Workers who did not work for Main-Line Railways

By Main-Line railways, I mean those railways generally of standard gauge which ran passenger and goods services available to the general public. Generally, the records included in the RAIL class at TNA are for those railway companies which provided public services.

I have not covered the hundreds of small railway operations run to move materials within factory complexes. These range from substantial networks around the breweries in Burton on Trent, and in the ironstone workings in Northamptonshire, with fleets of locomotives, through a line connecting two paper mills near Sittingbourne in Kent down to a single steam engine shunting wagons around a small factory, possibly not even connected to a Main-Line railway company. Many were built to standard gauge, but others were built to a narrow gauge. Any staff records for any of these operations would be in the records for the business concerned if they have survived.

If a person did not work for a railway company, it would be necessary to find where, if anywhere, records for the employer are held. Many people who worked 'on the railway' were not actually employed by a railway company. If you look around a modern railway station, there are many examples of

non-railway people employed on the station by newsagents, catering stalls, and many other types of retail outlet. This has been the case for most of the history of the railways.

Almost all the major new construction works were carried out by the big civil engineering companies. In view of the fact that most of the labour force were 'casual' employees, few records were ever made except in the gangers' notebooks. I suspect where records were made at the time of employment, these were kept locally and destroyed once the contract was completed and payment made. My experience in recent times suggests that the record keeping in respect of staff histories for contract staff was rudimentary, and I have no reason to suppose that the 19th century record keeping was any better.

CHAPTER SEVENTEEN
Overseas Railways

Whilst I have intentionally ignored overseas railways, the same basic principles for tracing people will still apply, although there may be problems of distance and language to be overcome.

A number of railways around the world were built by British labour and effectively were owned by companies linked to the U.K. This applies to the British Empire in the 19th century, and most railways in the parts of the world coloured red on the maps of the period were constructed and managed by British managers and engineers. The indigenous labour was gradually trained to do the dirtier and harder jobs.

One area outside the Empire where there was significant British influence was in South America, especially in Chile, Uruguay and Argentina. In this corner of the world, expatriate staff formed communities, and staff from English companies would gain experience by working there and then returning to Britain.

A listing of a large number of overseas railways in Africa, India, Australasia, North and South America arranged by country can be found in the issues of the Railway Year Book. A copy of the 1922 issue of the Year Book was on a CD distributed with Issue no 74 of Your Family Tree for March 2009.

GLOSSARY OF TERMS

In this section, I have attempted to give a list of the commoner staff grades and terminology that might be encountered when looking at railway records. The list is by no means complete, but should help understanding of the records and books.

To keep the list to manageable proportions, I have not included terms like labourer, bricklayer, blacksmith, carpenter and joiner which have the same meaning on and off the railway. Nor have I attempted to include railway slang, as this is unlikely to appear in the official records.

Big Four: These were the four railway companies formed in 1923: viz Great Western Railway; London Midland & Scottish Railway; London & North Eastern Railway and Southern Railway.

Boilersmith/Boilermaker: The person responsible for inspection and minor repairs to locomotive boilers at a locomotive shed. In a major works, would undertake fabrication and installation of new boilers as well as repairs.

Booking Clerk: Originally passengers were booked in a large ledger, and a receipt was given to the passenger. Thomas Edmondson, a booking clerk on the Newcastle & Carlisle Railway devised a system of sequentially numbered card tickets which could be given to the passenger.

Booking lad: A boy who was employed in busy signal boxes to record the movements of trains and the times bell signals were sent to adjacent signal boxes. Sometimes, Signalmen and others who were unfit for normal duties would be appointed as booking lads.

C & W: Carriage and Wagon.

Carman: A man riding on a horse drawn cart and employed to handle the parcels.

Carriage & Wagon Examiner: A person employed to carry out examination of trains at terminal stations and junctions. Might be called to attend incidents where trains had developed defects en-route. They would generally be expected to undertake minor repairs sufficient to get the train back to a depot.

Carter: The man driving a horse drawn cart, generally working from a station or Goods' Depot, delivering and collecting parcels that were conveyed by train for some of their journey. Generally stayed with the cart to look after the horses.

Chargehand: A railway term for what, in outside industry, would be called a foreman. Mainly used in the engineering sections.

Cleaner: As well as the general definition, in a railway context this refers to a man who carried out cleaning of steam locomotives. Was generally the first rung on the promotional ladder to becoming a Fireman and then Driver.

Crossing: There are three railway definitions;

1. An abbreviation for level crossing;
2. The intersection of two tracks which crossed at an angle;
3. The ironwork where two tracks crossed at an angle – either fabricated from rails or made as a single piece in a foundry.

Crossing Keeper: A person in attendance at a level crossing to operate the gates to allow road traffic to cross the railway. Usually would be in communication with the Signalman to ascertain that the line was clear for vehicles to cross the line.

Diagram: A listing of the duties to be carried out by a railwayman (generally a member of train crew) or by a locomotive or set of coaches.

Detonators: See Fog Signals.

Driver: In a railway context this term almost invariably means the driver of a steam engine, who is responsible for observing and reacting to all signals, He will have been promoted from Fireman.

Fireman: In a railway context this generally means the man who stokes the fire on a steam engine. He will have been promoted from a Cleaner and can expect in the fullness of time to be promoted to Driver.

Firewood Order: A railway worker could apply for an allocation of scrap timber from time to time; this might be offcuts from a saw mill or scrap railway sleepers. It was the responsibility of the employee to collect the timber and take it home.

Fitter: This term is a general one for any man who carries out repairs to mechanical equipment, such as locomotives, carriages, wagons, mechanical plant and signalling equipment.

Fog Signalling: During conditions of fog, a reduction in the speed and number of trains was necessary. At certain signals, to assist drivers to see the signals, Fog Signalmen would be appointed to replicate the signal indication using flags or lights.

Fog-Signalman: This would be a member of the local Permanent Way gang, who would be called out after normal hours, or redirected from his normal duties to work at a signal during fog or falling snow. In those weather conditions the gangs could not work on the tracks safely, and had a rhyme 'in fog or falling snow into the hut you will go', so they were available. The fogsignalman would place 'fog signals' on the rail to alert an approaching Driver that he was approaching a signal.

Fog Signals: A small explosive charge in a metal case, which can be clipped to the rail to warn locomotive drivers, during fog or in any emergency as laid down in the Railway Rule Book.

Free Passes: These were tickets issued for leisure travel. The number of passes granted annual was related to the grade of the employee, and would generally include the wife and children of the employee. Normally use was restricted to the lines and trains of the employing company.

Ganger: The man in charge of a gang undertaking track maintenance and renewal. A Ganger at a rural station might have a Sub-Ganger and half a dozen men, whereas a Ganger responsible for maintaining a few miles of a main line could have a couple of sub-gangers and a dozen men. A Ganger would report to the local Permanent Way Inspector. The track maintenance equivalent of a Chargehand.

Gauge: In a railway context this is the distance between the inside faces of the rail. There are three classifications of gauge:

1. Standard Gauge: First adopted by George Stephenson in 1825 for the Stockton and Darlington Railway. Reputed to be based on the distance between wheels used on the wagonways in Northumberland. 4ft 8½ins or 1432mm used today. Used around the world.

2. Broad Gauge: Strictly any width greater than the Standard Gauge, but generally used in Britain to mean the unique gauge of 7ft 0¼ inches, designed by Isambard Kingdom Brunel for the Great Western Railway. Irish, Spanish and some Australian Railways use 5ft 3in.

3. Narrow Gauge: Any gauge less than the Standard Gauge – typically might be 3ft, 2ft 3in (Talyllyn Railway in Wales), 2ft (Ffestiniog Railway in North Wales), or even 15 inch (Romney, Hythe & Dymchurch Railway and Ravenglass & Eskdale Railway). 3ft 6in gauge is used in New Zealand and South Africa.

Goods' Agent: The manager in charge of a goods' depot. Often responsible in small towns for soliciting trade for the railway. Can also be employed in a town office to arrange for the collection and delivery of goods and parcels to the local shops.

Grouping: The merging of the railways into 4 large companies set up under the powers of the Railway Act 1921, coming into effect at 12:01 am on 1 January 1923.

Guard: The person responsible for a train. On passenger trains may also inspect tickets and look after parcels and luggage in his compartment. The term dates from the stagecoach days. Where no shunter was available, he would couple and uncouple carriages and wagons, and, at small stations, direct the locomotive crew about the positioning of wagons for loading and unloading.

Hand Signalman: A person who works in place of fixed signals, under the instructions of a Signalman. The indications are given by flags, or, at night, by lamps.

Inspector: A supervisor, in any department. A Permanent Way Inspector, for example would be responsible for 50 or so miles of track, with around 12 gangs and 100 men. At a major station there would be one or two Station Inspectors on each turn. Permanent Way Inspectors would have a team of 15 or so Gangers covering the Inspectors area as well as 2 or 3 Sub-Inspectors.

Knocker Up: A man, or boy, employed at a locomotive shed, to go round to the houses of drivers and firemen to wake them for their next turn of duty or to advise them of changed arrangements.

Knowledge of the Road: Firemen, drivers and guards were required to have an intimate knowledge of the lines over which they worked trains. This included the exact position of signals, and points along with physical features such as tunnels and gradients. They were required to sign that they knew each individual route. This record would be retained at the depot to assist in allocating duties to those men that had 'signed' for the route.

L.C.&W: Locomotive, Carriage & Wagon: the department responsible for all activities connected with the maintenance of the trains themselves.

Length: A section of route where the tracks are maintained by a number of Lengthmen under the control of a Ganger.

Lengthman: A member of a length gang carrying out day to day track maintenance on a length of track.

Level Crossing: A place where a road or farm track crosses the railway on the level. The gates might be worked by a crossing keeper, or by a signalman, or even, where there was little rail and road traffic, by road users themselves.

Link: see Top Link.

Local Departmental Committee (LDC): A joint forum with representatives from both management and staff sides. The LDC would meet regularly or as required to sort out local problems and agree changes to the rostering. Typically the average locomotive shed would have two or three elected representatives of the Drivers and Firemen and would meet the Shedmaster and his assistant. LDC or similar arrangements were in place for all types of staff below management. Came into being in the 1920s after the trade union movement had started. Matters unresolved at LDC level would be elevated to the appropriate Sectional Council. It would be rare that a paid trade union official attended meetings.

Locomotive Shed: A covered area with associated sidings where locomotives were cleaned, refuelled and tanks replenished with water. The fitters and boilersmiths would carry out inspection of the arriving locomotives to ensure they were still 'fit for purpose'. At most sheds, one or two covered sidings would be set aside for the fitters and boilersmiths to carry out minor repairs. In some sheds the coaling would be undertaken from a large hopper rising 60 feet from ground level, containing hundreds of tons of coal.

Main Line Railways: The term is used to mean those railways which merged into the Big Four groups in 1923. Generally, they used the Stephenson, or Standard Gauge, of 4ft 8½ins. The Great Western Railway, the Bristol & Exeter and Cornwall Railways among others used the Brunel 7ft gauge until the final conversion to Standard Gauge in 1892, but were always classed as Main-Line.

Mixed Train: A train carrying passengers but with a number of non-passenger wagons attached at the rear.

Motor Driver: A man who drives a Road Motor.

Mutual Improvement Class (MIC): A self education group for enabling junior locomotive staff to gain the knowledge of the working of the locomotive, its brakes and the railway rule book. All the training was carried out in their own time, led by senior Drivers or locomotive Inspectors, who would demonstrate the workings of a locomotive either using models or on a locomotive in the shed. The classes were supported by the railway companies, who would often supply models of valve gear and the braking system for the class. The companies understood the benefit of having a well trained workforce.

Nationalisation: The creation of a single railway under the powers of the Transport Act 1947, came into effect at 12:01 am on 1 January 1948. This single railway was initially called the Railway Executive of the British Transport Commission, but became British Railways in 1962.

Navvy/Navvies: An abbreviation for navigators who were the men that moved the earth for the construction of canals. As railways took over from canals the term continued to be used for the men who moved the earth from cuttings and tipped it on embankments.

Number taker: A person employed to record the numbers of wagons and carriages passing over lines connecting one company to another. Generally, was employed by the Railway Clearing House, rather than individual railway companies.

Passed Cleaner: A cleaner who has passed the examination for Fireman and was available to be used on Fireman's Duties.

Passed Fireman: A fireman who has passed the examination for Driver, and was available for use on Driver's duties.

Permanent Way (PW or P Way): The rails, sleepers and fastenings, supported by stone ballast. So called because it replaced the temporary way used by the navvies constructing the railway. Actually the track needs partial renewal of components every 10-15 years, and full renewal every 20 years on main lines or 50 years on branch lines.

Platelayer: Originally was used for the men who laid the plateways, but became a general term for the men who maintained the track.

Plater: A man who laid out the plates for fabrication of girders and steelwork ready for drilling and riveting into the form set out in the drawings.

Plateway: A primitive form of railway, using 'L' shaped iron plates and wagons with flangeless wheels to transport goods over distance of no more than a maximum of five to ten miles. Generally any trains would be hauled by men or horses.

Points: Moveable rails controlled by a signalbox (or, in goods' yards, a hand lever) to enable trains to cross from one track to another, or to take a branch line.

Porter: A person employed at a station or goods' depot to carry parcels and passengers' luggage. They would also be carrying out the general sweeping and cleaning around the station. Another part of their duties was to generally assist and direct passengers. At smaller stations when no booking clerk or ticket collector was on duty, a porter would undertake those functions.

Porter/Signalman: A person employed to do the duties of both a Porter and Signalman, generally would be a Porter for most of a turn of duty, but would be the Signalman for a few hours to fill a planned gap in the roster. Mostly found at small stations on rural lines, where the traffic was light.

Post-Grouping: In railway history refers to the period between 1923 and 1947.

Pre-Grouping: In railway history refers to before 1923.

Privilege Ticket: A ticket issued to railway staff and their dependants at ¼ of the public ordinary single or return. Staff had to apply for the tickets. The application form was countersigned by or on behalf of the local manager before presentation to the Booking Office. Tickets issued for travel over the lines of another company were sometimes called 'foreign' tickets.

Relief Staff: These were men employed to cover absence of men on holiday or sick. Generally relief men were only found as Signalmen, Booking Clerks and Traffic Department Inspectors. They would be paid an enhanced rate for their knowledge of a wide area. A Relief Signalman might be expected to know between 12 and 20 signal boxes in such detail that he could take over at short notice. There were spare men employed as porters and clerks, but their duties did not require detailed knowledge of the working of trains and stations.

Rivetter: A man who hammered red hot iron rivets into preformed holes to join plates together with overlapping joints. A Rivetter's Mate would heat the rivets and throw them up to a second mate who would place the rivet in the hole for the riveter to hammer home.

Road Motor: The railway term for a motor lorry.

Road Knowledge: see Knowledge of the Road.

Running Foreman: Responsible for organising locomotives and their crews during a shift on an hour-by-hour basis. Often this would be a driver who had been promoted, but there were a number of cases where a fitter who had demonstrated management skills would be promoted into the post.

S & T: Signal and Telegraph. This title survived until around 1990 when it changed to Signal and Telecommunication.

Sectional Council (SC): A meeting between union officials and railway management to discuss industrial relations problems. Came into being with the growth of the trade union movement on the railways in the 1920s.

Shedmaster: The Manager in charge of a Locomotive Shed; frequently the post was filled by young mechanical engineers at the start of their career.

Shunter: Carried out coupling and uncoupling of carriages and wagons. In the bigger goods depots, they would direct the movements of locomotives to place wagons in the correct places for loading or unloading. In big goods sorting yards they would run alongside the moving wagons to apply the brakes.

Signalman: The person who works in a signal box or signal cabin to control the movements of trains. At junctions would be responsible for operating the levers to move the points to enable trains to take alternative routes as well as operating the signals. Often referred to as a 'bobby' in recognition of signalling being one of the tasks initially entrusted to the Railway Police, although this slang is rarely used today. For safety reasons, he had to be passed annually as competent to work a particular box. This would be done by a Signalling Inspector.

Sleepers: The timber beams at right angles to and under the rails. The timbers were treated by pressure impregnation with creosote among other places at works near Darlington and at Ditton, Taunton and Southampton. Concrete sleepers only came into being, initially in sidings, in the 1930s.

Slip Carriage: A coach which was detached from a non-stop train to give a service to an intermediate station. After detachment, a slip guard would control the braking of the coach.

Station Master: A manager who was in charge of the day to day activities with a station and its railway environs.

Sub-Ganger: Assistant to a Ganger. He would sometimes be responsible for undertaking the daily track patrol looking for defects in the track, fencing and banks.

Sub-Inspector: Assistant to an Inspector in any department.

Telegraph: An electrical communication system using either a pair of needles or Morse Code to transmit messages from place to place. A telegraph instrument would be sited in major stations, with a trained clerk in attendance to take down and send messages. Most railways identified stations by a two (or sometimes three) letter code, and this code is still in use today for written notes and summaries of events, particularly by older staff. Typical examples that I can recall are VA for Victoria, IG for Brighton and BZ for Bexleyheath. These codes may be encountered in operating publications, such as the weekly and daily traffic notices detailing short term changes to the timetable. The telegraph was gradually superseded by telephone and then fax and, today, e-mail.

Ticket Collector: Employed at medium and large stations to check the tickets of all passengers going onto or leaving the platforms.

Timekeeper: A key person in a station or depot, who would record the times men booked on and off duty and compiled the time sheet. Was frequently a man who had had to be taken off normal duties due to ill health or injury.

Top Link: The most senior group of Drivers numbering 12- 20 at a shed. They would work round the turns allocated to the link in rotation. The top link would work the most prestigious trains – at Kings Cross shed, the top link men would work the fast trains north along the East Coast main line to Grantham, Doncaster, Leeds, York or even Newcastle, handing over an Edinburgh bound train to a top link man from Newcastle or Edinburgh. Each driver would have his regular Fireman. A series of links would exist at each shed covering all the workings needed down to the shed link made up of either very new drivers or those who were not fit for Main Line duty. As a Driver gained experience, he would be promoted up through the links as vacancies arose.

Town Office: Railway premises away from a station to provide a local collection point for parcels to be forwarded from the traders in the town.

Turn (or Turn of Duty): The railway term for a shift. Early turn starts between 3 and 7 am, late turn starts between noon and 3 pm and night turn starts at around 10 pm. However, train crew, such as Drivers, Guards and Firemen might start their turn at any time, as required to be on duty to work the trains. Inspectors, signalmen, and maintenance staff in depots would either work days (starting at 7 or 8 am) or start their turn at 6 am, 2 pm or 10pm once the 8 hour day had come into effect.

Wagonway: see Plateway

Washer out: A man in a locomotive shed who drained the boiler of every locomotive on a weekly or two-weekly cycle to wash out dirt from the boiler.

Water Troughs: A facility whereby locomotives could take on water without stopping, using scoops lowered by the locomotive crew.

Wheel Tapper: To be seen at stations walking beside a train with a long handled hammer tapping the wheels to check that the tyres were sound. A ringing sound indicated all was well, while a dull thud indicated that the tyre was broken and the vehicle would have to be taken out of service. The man performing this duty would be a Carriage and Wagon Examiner.

Working Timetable: The timetable that shows all scheduled trains, passenger and freight, giving the times at which they are timed to pass key locations as well as any stopping points. Generally times are shown to the half minute. On single lines, the book will also specify where trains are to meet and pass each other in passing places (loops).

BIBLIOGRAPHY

This section contains a selection of books that I hope will provide background material to help in your research, such as maps, but, more importantly, will enable you to see where the individual fitted into the whole organisation and what his work entailed.

There are two publishers who have specialised in histories of smaller railways and branch lines and I have not attempted to list their books:

Oakwood Press Many of their books are out of print but may be found in secondhand railway booksellers advertising in the railway enthusiast press. They have also published a number of books about the careers of a number of Locomotive Engineers – including Lawson Billington, D Earle Marsh, the Drummond brothers, C B Collett, R E L Maunsell, Vincent Raven. All have family details as well as dealing with the professional career of the subject and technical matters.

Middleton Press are gradually producing a series of picture albums for a line or group of lines. The books contain pictures of stations and reproductions of Ordnance Survey maps of stations. Each book contains about one hundred photographs of the line concerned. Whilst rarely showing staff, it is possible to obtain an idea of the station premises where an ancestor worked. Started with lines in Southern England, but have extended into the Midlands, West Country and Wales.

General Books

Note All the books listed that were published before the end of 1995 will be found listed in the Ottley Bibliographies.

Was Your Grandfather a Railwayman? by Tom Richards (Author and Federation of Family History Societies 4th Edition 2002). The definitive listing of all known railway staff records including some overseas railway companies, mainly in the Commonwealth. (Reprint expected in 2009/10).

A Bibliography of Railway History by George Ottley (Volume 1, George Allen & Unwin 1965, 2nd edition HMSO 1983; Volume 2, Supplement 7951-12956 HMSO 1988 plus Second Supplement 12957-19605 National Railway Museum with Railway & Canal Historical Society). A very comprehensive listing of books of which the first volume was compiled by a member of staff at the then British Museum Library and extended in date range subsequently by others.

Railway Ancestors - a Guide to the Staff Records of the Railway Companies of England and Wales 1822-1947 by David Hawkins (Alan Sutton and Public Record Office 1995 - 2nd revised edition 2008). Deals principally with the railway staff records held by the National Archives, although there are some references to other archives.

Railway Records: a Guide to Sources by Cliff Edwards (Public Record Office 2001).

Railwaywomen: exploitation, betrayal and triumph in the workplace by Helena Wojtczak (Hastings Press 2005). The story of women workers on the railway.

The Railway Navvies by Terry Coleman (Hutchinson 1965, reprinted Pimlico 2000). This gives a good description of the general living conditions and methods of working of the men who built the railways.

A Regional History of the Railways of Great Britain in 14 volumes by various authors (David & Charles 1960-1975). Provides a general history of Britain's railways outlining their development, and gives an overview of their construction and mergers.

Fire & Steam by Christian Wolmar (Atlantic Books 2008) (p/b) This is a wide ranging railway history looking at how the coming of the railways transformed Britain.

For the King's Service – Railway Ships at War by A J Mullay (Pendragon Press 2008). An account of the railway ships that were called up for service during the World Wars.

The Fair Sex – Women and the Great Western Railway by Rosa Matheson (Tempus Publishing 2007). Although focussing on one railway, this book illustrates the work of women on the railway, with many illustrations of the women and some of the paperwork associated with their employment.

The Railway Dictionary by Alan A Jackson (Alan Sutton 2006 (4th Edition). Covers railway terminology and slang world-wide.

A Gazetteer of the Railway Contractors and Engineers by Lawrence Popplewell (Melledgen Press 1982-89) in 10 volumes covering the regions of Britain. Details the contractors and engineers for each line in chronological order. (Approx. 50 pages each volume, thin card covers).

Personal stories

Over the years many books of reminiscences have been published, but most have been by men who were Drivers and Firemen.

I have listed a few books by railwaymen of various grades which give good descriptions of the work and conditions post 1948, but with relevance to earlier eras. They can be useful to understand the type of work that the various grades undertook and their relationship with other workers. Even the Managers included in the list started their careers at Supervisory or junior management level

Proceed at Caution by Peter Kirton (Challenger UK 1998). Describes his career from Signalman through Travelling Ticket Inspector to a Chief Inspector handling, among other things, movements of the Royal Family by ordinary trains.

I Tried to Run a Railway by Gerard Fiennes (Ian Allan 1967). Covers his career from Clerk in the 1930s through the operational line of promotion to General Manager in the 1960s.

Birmingham Engineman by Dennis Herbert (Oakwood Press 2007). Describes the work of a locomotive man from leaving school to Main Line Driver.

From Steam to Stone – a BR Life by David Butcher (Oakwood Press 2004 in 2 volumes) Describes a career from engine cleaner to management, with accounts of the training and industrial relations aspects of the later stages of his career.

Mind the Doors by Robert Griffith (Silver Link Publishing 2002). An account of working on the London Underground, both on stations and as a Guard and Driver.

Articles in the family history press

A selection of articles from 2008 are listed, but others have been published in earlier years

- ◆ '*British Transport Police*'; in *Family Tree Magazine* Oct 2008.

- ◆ '*Best Website for Researching Railway Ancestors*'; In *Who Do You Think You Are?* Issue 14 (October 2008). Almost all the sites listed will only give general historical background to your ancestors' working lives.

- ◆ '*Railway Records*'; In *Your Family Tree* Issue No 70 November 2008.

Websites

Due to the rapidly changing scene, rather than listing sites at the time of writing, I strongly advise using a search engine such as Google to search for sites relating to the particular railway of interest to you to get the most up to date information.

Magazines

Railway Gazette. A magazine directed towards the professional railway manager with detailed descriptions of new rolling stock, station and signalling layouts. However, there also are potted biographies of senior staff.

Railway Magazine. Published since 1897. Until the 1980s, had a range of articles on all topics, including railway operation and history and particularly before 1948, biographies of staff, often managers who had been promoted or were retiring, but some Top Link Drivers. More recently, the articles have shown a trend to being much less historically based.

Backtrack. Started publication in the 1990s. Tends to specialise in general history of particular section of lines, but articles do refer to individuals from time to time. Over the years has had articles describing the actual construction of lines with diagrammatic maps. Copiously illustrated, with photographs often showing the railway in the landscape.

British Railways Illustrated. Similar to Backtrack, but the maps are generally reproduced from the Ordnance Survey. Tends to specialise in the history of locomotive depots, but covers other topics as well and features good illustrations of railway depots and stations from 1900 to around 1970. In many of the articles there are reproductions of an Ordnance Survey map of the area.

Steam World. Started publication in the 1980s and has had a number of articles written by retired railwaymen about parts of their careers, mostly about the period from 1940 to 1970.

Atlases and Maps

Pre-Grouping Atlas and Gazetteer (Ian Allan Ltd). Shows the railway system at 1922, with lines and stations marked with the owning/operating company.

A Complete Atlas of Railway Station Names by Tony Dewick (Ian Allan Ltd 2002). An atlas based on the Pre-grouping Atlas and Gazetteer, but listing all the changes of name of railway stations.

The Railways of Great Britain – A Historical Atlas by Col. M H Cobb (2 volumes, Ian Allan 2004). This is undoubtedly the best historical atlas ever produced for the railways of England, Scotland and Wales. In some 680 pages of maps, the railways are shown in colour superimposed on grey and white 1 inch Ordnance Survey maps. Stations and junctions are all named, and the names of the railway companies are shown in bold type, with dates of merger or take-over. Included are a series of charts showing the mergers, take-overs and amalgamations (with dates) for each of the Big Four.

Railways of Britain by Colin and David McCarthy (Ian Allan Ltd 2006 onwards). This is a series of atlas books, each of which covers one or two counties showing all railways known to have been constructed. So far Norfolk & Suffolk; Kent & Sussex and Devon & Cornwall have been published. The maps are derived from the work done by Col. Cobb.

Alan Godfrey Maps. These are available from the publisher Alan Godfrey by mail order or through the Internet. (You need to be certain that the street you want is on the map you order). Alternatively, there are stands at some family history fairs where a selection of the maps is on sale. Local bookshops often carry a small selection of maps of their locality. Ian Allan Bookshops also carry a small range of the maps.

Where to get railway books and magazines

Current copies of magazines are available from most newsagents but may need to be specially ordered outside large towns. Regrettably, it seems that the wholesalers are demanding larger scale sales before they will supply a magazine, of whatever subject, to newsagents for display on the shelves. If you want isolated issues, the publishers may be able to supply back numbers, and the current issues are available from the Ian Allan Bookshops in London (Lower Marsh near Waterloo Station), at Manchester Piccadilly (in the Station Approach), in Central Cardiff (in Royal Arcade) and in Central Birmingham (Stephenson Street).

The Ian Allan bookshops also carry a wide stock of books in print, as well as magazines, covering all forms of transport.

Another specialist shop is Motor Books at Cecil Court, off Charing Cross Road, who carry a selection of transport books including railways, and current issues of overseas railway periodicals.

Robert Humm at Stamford, in the station buildings, carries some new books and a very large stock of second-hand books on railways. Humm also stocks complete volumes of most of the railway periodicals, but single issues may be difficult to obtain as the main market within the railway enthusiast world is for complete annual volumes.

Other second hand booksellers advertise in the railway press, notably the Railway Magazine from time to time.

Some of the private railways around the country have a railway bookshop and if there is one of these operations near you, this may be a good source of books and magazines.

Most public libraries should be able to obtain a copy of the books listed, and some may be held by Reference or Local Studies Libraries. The National Railway Museum at York should have copies of some of the works that are listed and these will be found in the Search Engine section of the Museum on the Mezzanine floor in the Great Hall.

INDEX

Founded in 1911 the Society of Genealogists (SoG) is Britain's premier family history organisation. The Society maintains a splendid genealogical library and education centre in Clerkenwell.

The Society's collections are particularly valuable for research before the start of civil registration of births marriages and deaths in 1837 but there is plenty for the beginner too. Anyone starting their family history can book free help sessions in the open community access area where free help can be given in searching online census indexes or looking for entries in birth, death and marriage indexes.

The Library contains Britain's largest collection of parish register copies, indexes and transcripts and many nonconformist registers. Most cover the period from the sixteenth century to 1837. Along with registers, the library holds local histories, copies of churchyard gravestone inscriptions, poll books, trade directories, census indexes and a wealth of information about the parishes where our ancestors lived.

Unique indexes include Boyd's Marriage Index with more than 7 million names compiled from 4300 churches between 1538-1837 and the Bernau Index with references to 4.5 million names in Chancery and other court proceedings. Also available are indexes of wills and marriage licences, and of apprentices and masters (1710-1774). Over the years the Society has rescued and made available records discarded by government departments and institutions but of great interest to family historians. These include records from the Bank of England, Trinity House and information on Teachers and Civil Servants.

Boyd's and other unique databases are published on line on www.origins.com, on www.findmypast.com and on the Society's own website www.sog.org.uk . There is free access to these and many other genealogical sites within the Library's Internet suite.

The Society is the ideal place to discover if a family history has already been researched with its huge collection of unique manuscript notes, extensive collections of past research and printed and unpublished family histories. If you expect to be carrying out family history research in the British Isles then membership is very worthwhile although non-members can use the library for a small search fee.

The Society of Genealogists is an educational charity. It holds study days, lectures, tutorials and evening classes and speakers from the Society regularly speak to groups around the country. The SoG runs workshops demonstrating computer programs of use to family historians. A diary of events and booking forms are available from the Society on 020 7553 3290 or on the website www.sog.org.uk .

Members enjoy free access to the Library, certain borrowing rights, free copies of the quarterly *Genealogists Magazine* and various discounts of publications, courses, postal searches along with free access to data on the members' area of our website and each quarter to our data on www.origins.com.

More details about the Society can be found on its extensive website at www.sog.org.uk

For a free Membership Pack contact the Society at:

14 Charterhouse Buildings,
Goswell Road,
London EC1M 7BA
Telephone 020 7553 3291
Fax 020 7250 1800

The Society is always happy to help with enquiries and the following contacts may be of assistance.

Library & shop hours:

Monday	Closed
Tuesday	10am - 6pm
Wednesday	10am - 6pm
Thursday	10am - 8pm
Friday	Closed
Saturday	10am - 6pm
Sunday	Closed

Contacts:

Membership
Tel: 020 7553 3291
Email: membership@sog.org.uk

Lectures & courses
Tel: 020 7553 3290
Email: events@sog.org.uk

Family history advice line
Tel: 020 7490 8911
See website for availability

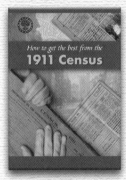
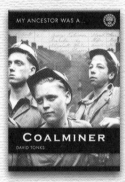